BIZARRE BOOKS

BIZARRE BOOKS

Russell Ash and Brian Lake

MACMILLAN

First published 1985 by
MACMILLAN LONDON LIMITED
4 Little Essex Street London WC2R 3LF
and Basingstoke

Associated companies in Auckland, Delhi, Dublin,
Gaborone, Hamburg, Harare, Hong Kong,
Johannesburg, Kuala Lumpur, Lagos, Manzini,
Melbourne, Mexico City, Nairobi, New York,
Singapore and Tokyo.

Typeset by Rowland Phototypesetting Ltd/
Bury St Edmunds, Suffolk

Printed by St Edmundsbury Press,
Bury St Edmunds, Suffolk

British Library Cataloguing in Publication Data

Bizarre books.
1. Books
I. Ash, Russell   II. Lake, Brian
002   Z4

ISBN 0-333-38312-5

Contents

To *the memory of Berthold Laufer (1874–1934), who did so much to add to the bibliography of bizarre books.*

Introduction

Every year since 1978 *The Bookseller* – "The Organ of the Book Trade" – and a
company called The Diagram Group have organized a competition at the time of
the Frankfurt Book Fair. A prize is awarded to the finder of the book title that
"most outrageously exceeds all bounds of credibility". The winners have been:

1978: **Proceedings of the Second International Workshop on
Nude Mice**

1979: **The Madam as Entrepreneur: Career Management in
House Prostitution**

1980: **The Joy of Chickens**

1981: **Last Chance at Love – Terminal Romances**

1982: *Judges split between*
Population and Other Problems
and
Braces Owner's Manual

1983: **The Theory of Lengthwise Rolling**

1984: **The Book of Marmalade: Its Antecedents, Its History and
Its Role in the World Today**

Russell Ash won the 1980 competition and has been a runner-up on several
occasions. In 1983 he wrote an article for *The Bookseller* in which he cast a wider
historical net, scooping in some of the bizarre book titles of the past.

In 1982 Brian Lake was one of the organizers of a Dud Books of All Time show at
a major antiquarian book fair in York which received considerable press attention.

In 1983 we were introduced by a bookseller who was aware of the similarity of
our interests, and we decided, tentatively, that there "might be a book in it".
Fortunately, we found our enthusiasms were complementary: one of us has studied
the subject from the perspective of contemporary publishing and library resources;
the other has viewed it from the point of view of the antiquarian book trade.

Frankly, when we embarked on our book quest, neither of us had the faintest
idea of how extensive the field might be. Also, unfortunately, librarians have not
had the foresight to catalogue books under "bizarre", so it is not that easy to find
them. Articles we wrote on the subject for various journals soon confirmed, though,
that we were entering a vast and largely uncharted territory. Booksellers and
librarians, publishers and closet collectors began to write to us with cherished
examples; sub-sections began defining themselves (and, incidentally, the prices of
second-hand books with weird titles began to escalate). Chance contacts led us to
such invaluable sources as Judi Vernau, whose meticulous work in editing the
published catalogues of the British Library has led her to many remarkable
discoveries, and who has an unfailing eye for the odd.

1

But what is odd? It is quite clear that one person's bizarre book is another's bread and butter. We thought *Searching for Railway Telegraph Insulators* a hugely funny and esoteric title until a lecturer in electronics asked where he could get a copy of this key text.

The meaning of many words has changed, so perhaps we stand guilty of homophobia in selecting a number of titles that include "gay" or "queer", which we find childishly funny but which their authors clearly did not. Apart from gays, lepers and monopods take a bit of a bashing. Sorry.

Double-entendre book and music titles are, in our view, inherently funny and so are presented with little comment. Certain other kinds of bizarre books tend to benefit from explanation and are therefore summarized.

We confidently assert that there has never before been a book like this. Raymond George Lister's *Books at Bedtime* (Cambridge: Golden Head Press, 1953) is a slim but highly entertaining list of daft books that one's house guests might be surprised to discover beside their beds. But, in general, the various authors and contributors to the subject occasionally have hazy memories. We have been offered some quite remarkable book titles that on closer investigation have turned out to be less amusing, or fabrications, or, indeed, spoofs. Therefore certain rules have been followed: we have included only books that we either own or that we have checked in a library collection (principally the British Library and those catalogued in the American National Union Catalog). We have omitted fakes and any that we felt were deliberately contrived – and hence have sacrificed, for example, a rich vein of science-fiction titles (which we may make the subject of a future book).

Somehow, the British publishing industry contrives to produce about 40,000 new titles every year. Everyone involved in helping us to compile this book – authors, publishers, editors, librarians and booksellers – is aware of the often anguishing processes through which a book goes from its initial conception to its ultimate sale to a reader. So it is still astonishing to us that, although we find the books listed and described in the following pages funny in one way or another, at least a reasonable percentage of the people responsible for adding to the world's book mountain never batted an eyelid at them.

Since some readers may find their own books mentioned, there is one point that we would like to make clear: we believe there is undeliberate humour in certain names and titles, in books on extraordinary specializations and exotic theories, in books and printed music with *double-entendre* titles, and in novels with strange plots and often stranger publishers' blurbs. None of this is to say that these are *bad* books or even that their authors were in any sense misguided in writing them. Just because *we* find them odd does not mean that they did not sell magnificently, fill a gap in the market and receive enormous acclaim (though some were, of course, massively remaindered). We make no apologies for including any book (after all, anyone who chooses to write a book opens him or herself to review and criticism, good or bad), but of any sensitive souls who are distressed to find themselves lampooned, we ask forgiveness. We did it for the money and a laugh.

Notes
All books published in London unless otherwise stated.

n.d.: no date   n.p.: no publisher

Acknowledgements

Special credits:

The Bookdealer (for prompting contributions from book dealers)
The Bookseller (for support and publicity)
British Library Reading Room staff (for not giggling)
The Diagram Group (for inventing the Frankfurt Book Fair prize) and all contributors to the Frankfurt Book Fair prize
Pete Jermy (our leading "pulp" merchant)
Eric Korn (for generous contributions from an acknowledged expert on bizarre books – and especially for the "Top Ten Rhyming Titles/Authors")
Peter Miller (for pioneering work in organizing the Dud Books of All Time Show, and for introducing the authors to each other)
The Provincial Booksellers' Fairs Association (for recognizing that there are "dud" books)
Brian Staples (for his "Clippings Together")
Martin Stone (for some particularly novel suggestions)
Jeff Towns (for supplying "England's True Wealth" and for general help)
Judi Vernau (for supplying most of our "Names to Conjure With" and "Musical Interlude" titles)
Michael Zinman (for giving us access to his collection)

All the rest:

Anon. of Nottingham
Michael Baker
Robert Baldock
M. & M. Baldwin
Louis Baum
Robin de Beaumont
Simon Brett
A. J. Browning
Mark Bryant
Nigel Burwood
Iain Campbell
Pat Cassidy
Philip Chancellor
M. & B. Clapham
Stephen Clarke
Graham Cornish
Countryside Books
James Cummins
Richard Dalby
Paul Davies
Patrick Davis
Rebecca Dearman
Disley Bookshop

Driffield
Andrew Duckworth
Roy Eden
John Eggeling
Christopher Eley
Toby English
Len Evans
David Fielder
Fine Books Oriental
Tony Fothergill
Laurie E. Gage
Patrick Gallagher
Joseph L. Gardner
Malcolm Gerratt
David Gillham
Mike & Sue Goldmark
William Goodsir
Martin Greif
Liz Groves
E. Hallett
Lionel Halter
Sylvian Hamilton
Dave Harris

George G. Harris
Paul Harris
Chris Heppa
Bernard Higton
Bevis Hillier
David Holmes
Philip M. Hopper
Horsham Bookshop
D. F. Howard
Barry Humphries
Paul Hutchinson
C. Hyland
D. Jarvis
Christopher Johnson
Annette Jolly
Richard Glyn Jones
Martin Keene
George Kelsale
John Kinnane
Patty Lafferty
Adam Langland
Library Association
  Record

Raymond Lister
George Locke
John A. Lord
Loughborough
   Bookshop
Caroline Lucas
John Lyle
Ian Lynn
Maggs Bros.
Vivian T. Maisey
Jo Manning
Nell McCorry
R. McCutcheon
Rod Mead
A. Micallef Grimaud
S. P. Milanytch
John Miller
Brian Mills
Montpelier Books
Michael Moon
Charles Mortimer
G. Mosdell
Margaret Nangle
Janet Nassau
New York Public Library

Kent Nielsen
C. J. Phillips
Roy Pitches
Primrose Hill Books
The Printer's Devil
Michael Prowse
Professor Robert
   Rosenthal
Ruth Royce
Robert Rubin
Matthew Searle
Barry Shaw
M. Shearer
Peter Shellard
Leslie Sherlock
Stanley Shoop
Louis Simmonds
Mrs M. I. Simpson
Frank Smith
Helen Smith
Timothy d'Arch Smith
I. G. Sparkes
D. Spector
J. R. Sperr
John Spiers

David Stagg
Colin Stillwell
G. E. C. & R. N. Stone
Nigel Tattersfield
Phil Thredder
Brian Tomes
M. Treloar
Triangle
Christine Trollope
Morris Venables
John Walton
Philip Ward
Steve Weissman
Anabel Whittet
Avril Whittle
Nicholas Willmott
Alan Wilson
Philip Wilson
Gerry Wolstenholme
Charles B. Wood III
Les Wray
Robin Wright
Vivian Wright
Stephen Wycherley

Finally, our thanks to all at Macmillan for their help, and especially to Brenda Stephenson, who edited the book.

And our apologies to anyone inadvertently omitted.

I
They Didn't Really Mean It
Unintentional double-entendre titles

Women on the Job
Judith Buber Agassi
Lexington, Mass.: Lexington Books, 1979
A lively account of the activities of professional women.

The Hookers of Kew
Mea Allan
Michael Joseph, 1967
A revealing biography of the eminent family of botanists.

The Resistance of Piles to Penetration
Russell V. Allin
Spon, 1935
An important treatise on a common problem.

How It Was Done at Stow School
Anon.
Hamilton Adams, 1888 (2nd edition)
The author did not like the way it was done at all.

THE

RESISTANCE OF PILES TO PENETRATION

TOGETHER WITH

TABLES OF APPROXIMATE VALUES BASED ON THE HILEY FORMULA

WITH

A FOREWORD BY SIR CYRIL KIRKPATRICK
PAST PRESIDENT OF THE INSTITUTION OF CIVIL ENGINEERS

BY

RUSSELL V. ALLIN, M.Inst.C.E.

1935

An engineering solution to a medical condition.

Perverse Pussy
Anon.
Philadelphia, Pa.: American Sunday-School Union, 1869
The anonymous author of *The Leighton Children* (Philadelphia, Pa.: American Sunday-School Union, 1867) gives us inside information on a reluctant feline.

The Boy Fancier
Frank Townend Barton
Routledge; New York: E. P. Dutton, 1912
Tips on caring for domestic pets.

Enter Ye In
James Sidlow Baxter
Edinburgh: Marshall, Morgan & Scott, 1939
And after twenty-one years:

Going Deeper
Edinburgh: Marshall, Morgan & Scott, 1960

Couplings to the Khyber
Percy Stuart Attwood Berridge
Newton Abbot: David & Charles, 1969
Riveting tales of the railways.

"Green Balls". The Adventures of a Night Bomber
Paul Bewsher
Edinburgh and London: W. Blackwood & Sons, 1919

The Saddle of Queens
Lida Louise Bloodgood
J. A. Allen, 1959

Persevering Dick
Mary D. R. Boyd
Philadelphia, Pa.: Presbyterian Board of Publication, 1867
Richard's dogged determination does not go unrewarded.

Camping Out for Boy Scouts
Victor George de Freyne Bridges
C. A. Pearson, 1910

Queer Shipmates
Archibald Bruce Campbell
Phoenix House, 1962

Where to Say No
Rose Terry Cooke
Gall & Inglis, 1887
Miss Cooke lays down the law.

The Garden of Ignorance. The Experiences of a Woman in a Garden
Marion Cran
Herbert Jenkins, 1913
The author continues to lead us up the garden path in this down-to-earth series:

```
THE  GARDEN
OF IGNORANCE
THE  EXPERIENCES  OF
A WOMAN IN A GARDEN

BY
MRS.
MARION
CRAN
F.R.H.S.




WITH EIGHT
ILLUSTRATIONS




HERBERT  JENKINS  LIMITED
3 YORK STREET LONDON S.W.
```

The Garden of Experience
Herbert Jenkins, 1922
The Joy of the Ground
Herbert Jenkins, 1928
The Lusty Pal
Herbert Jenkins, 1930
The Story of My Ruin
Herbert Jenkins, 1924

The first book in Marion Cran's gardening series, published 1913–30, the titles of which tell an entirely different story.

Every Frenchman Has One
Olivia De Havilland
Paul Elek, 1963
The famous actress reveals what every Frenchwoman already knows.

Penetrating Wagner's Ring
John L. Di Gaetanao
New York: Da Capo, 1978
An in-depth study of the great composer's *Meisterwerk*.

The Pansy Books
Ida M. Loder Donisthorpe
G. Routledge, 1887–90 (27 vols.)
A comprehensive library of pansiana.

Making It in Leather
M. Vincent Hayes
New York: Drake, 1972; Newton Abbot: David & Charles, 1973

The Chronicles of the Crutch
Blanchard Jerrold
William Tinsley, 1860

Suggestive Thoughts for Busy Workers
J. Osborne Keen
Bible Christian Book Room, 1883

Gay Crusaders
Magdalen King-Hall
Peter Davies, 1934
Presents the Middle Ages in an entirely new light.

The Big Problem of Small Organs
Alan T. Kitley
Colchester: The Author, 1966
A key difficulty solved in a noteworthy book.

❛Having spent ten years devising schemes for the small organ I reluctantly decided that "there ain't no such animal", as a famous cowboy once said.❜

Mr Kitley then went away and wrote a book on it.

Explorations at Sodom
Melvin Grove Kyle
Religious Tract Society, 1928
Archaeological secrets uncovered.

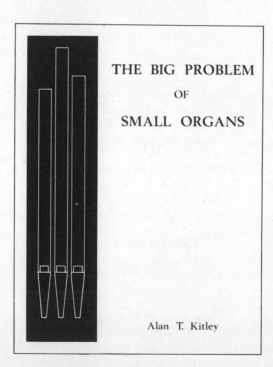

THE BIG PROBLEM

OF

SMALL ORGANS

Alan T. Kitley

The tone of this useful handbook on organic growth, published by the author and pitched at the disadvantaged, contradicts the often-stated assertion that size is not important.

How to Avoid Intercourse With Your Unfriendly Car Mechanic
Harold M. Landy
New York: Ashley Books, 1977
Service costs are high enough anyway; avoiding further complications will be welcomed by many motorists.

Memorable Balls
James Laver
Derek Verschoyle, 1954
The eminent art historian recalls some fashionable Society entertainments.

Briefs Calmly Considered
"A Layman"
York: A. Barclay, 1826
The anonymous author is unaroused by his subject.

Sods I Have Cut on the Turf
Jack Leach
Victor Gollancz, 1961

Shifts and Expedients of Camp Life
William Barry Lord and Thomas Baines
Horace Cox, 1871

The Midnight Cry; or, Signs in the Church of the Bridegroom's Second Coming
Revd J. Lowes
Carlisle: n.p., 1800
A sermon: "Fire from Heaven . . . has burnt up our natural *heavens* of joy and delight in the flesh".

Joyful Lays
Revd R. Lowry and W. Howard Doane
New York and Chicago: Biglow & Main, 1886

Queer Doings in the Navy
Asa M. Mattice
Cambridge, Mass.: Line Officers' Association, 1896

Little Lays for Little Lips
Helen J. A. Mills (illustrator)
William Wells Gardner, 1875 (3rd edition)
Featuring "The Foolish Chicken".

The Fags, and Other Poems
William Moore
Kegan Paul, Trench, Trübner, 1912

The Oldest Trade in the World, and Other Addresses for the Younger Folk
George H. Morrison
Oliphant, Anderson & Ferrier, 1898
A title in the *Golden Nails* series.

Tinklings from the Sheepfolds
Matthias Pearson*
Simpkin, Marshall & Co., 1871
(* The pseudonym of John William Fletcher.)
The author of *Flirtation; or, The Way into the Wilderness* (Robert Theobald, 1854) provides some interesting thoughts.

Scouts in Bondage
Geoffrey Prout
Aldine Publishing Co., 1930

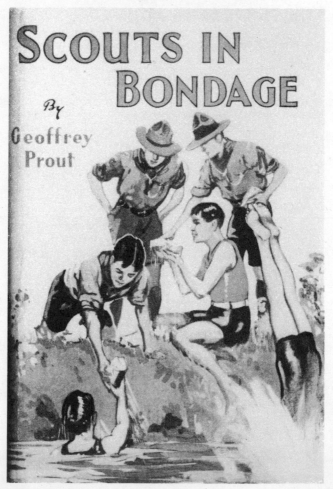

A well-bound copy of the book that goes some way to explaining the boy scout's obsession with ropes and knots.

10

What Was Said in the Woods
Gustav zu Putlitz
Longman, Brown, 1851

Camping Among Cannibals
Alfred St Johnston
Macmillan, 1883
Dangerous exploits by an eccentric explorer.

Under Two Queens
John Huntley Skrine
Macmillan, 1884

The Scrubber Strategy
Robert T. Stafford
New York: Harper & Row, 1982

Fifty Years with the Rod
John Stirling
Philip Allan, 1929
An exhausting half-century described by the president of the Scottish Anglers'
Association.

Keeping Your Tools Tiptop
Thomas Umpleby
Detroit, Mich.: The Author, 1954

The Gay Boys of Old Yale!
John Denison Vose
New Haven, Conn.: Hunter, c. 1869
Carefree varsity days recalled.

Organ Building for Amateurs
Mark Wicks
Ward Lock, 1887
A do-it-yourself guide to bigger and better organs.

And There I Stood with My Piccolo in My Hand
Meredith Willson
Garden City, NY: Doubleday, 1948; Westport, Conn.: Greenwood Press, 1976 (reprint)
The author of *The Music Man* and *What Every Young Musician Should Know*
(New York: Robbins, 1938) describes his most embarrassing moment.

2
The Name's the Same
Unlikely books by authors with the same names as the famous and infamous

R. Ash
How to Write a Tax Brief
Englewood Cliffs, NJ: Prentice-Hall, 1936

Richard Baker
Famous Trees of New Zealand
George Ronald, 1965 (Vol. 2 in the Famous Tree Library*)*

Ronnie Barker
Tendency to Corrupt, A Novel
Cassell, 1957

Alan Bennet
Outlook for the Small Business
Birmingham: Bow Group Pamphlets, 1961

George Best
Morality and Utility: a Natural Science of Ethics
Trübner & Co., 1887

G. Boycott
Compressed Airwork and Diving
C. Lockwood, 1909

Richard Burton
Youth's Divine Pastime . . . Containing Scripture Histories Turned into English Verse
C. Hitch & J. Hodges, 1749

James Cagney*
The Throat and Nose
Baillière, Tindall & Cox, 1899
(*Contributor of the section on nervous diseases in the fifth edition.)

Charles Chaplin
Ornamental Lathework for Amateurs
P. Marshall, 1914

Joan Collins
A New Look at Social Work
Pitman, 1967

Peter Cook
The Calculation of Load and Torque in Hot Flat Rolling
British Iron & Steel Association, 1958

J. R. Ewing
Public Service of Jacob Dolson Cox
Washington, DC: Neale Publishing Co., 1902

Dr Frankenstein
The Roots of the Ego. A Phenomenology of Dynamics and of Structure
Baltimore, Md.: Williams & Wilkins, 1966

D. Frost
An Address Delivered Before the Canterbury Temperance Society
Brooklyn, Conn.: n.p., 1829

Billy Graham
Smoke Abatement in Manchester
Manchester: J. E. Cornish, 1896

Benny Green
How to Pay Off the National Debt
Philadelphia, Pa.: Claxton, Remsden & Haffelfinger, 1872

Edward Heath
Vaccination; or, Blood Poisoning with Animal Diseases
Heath & Co., 1898

Benny Hill
The Moral Responsibility of Civil Rulers
Hartford, Conn.: Printed by C. Babcock, 1829

Sherlock Holmes
Sales Course for Retail Assistants
Johannesburg: South African Photographic Trade Association, 1962

Robin Hood
Industrial Social Security in the South
Chapel Hill, NC: University of North Carolina Press, 1936

Bob Hope
Mediaeval Music: an Historical Sketch
Elliot Stock, 1899 (2nd edition)

B. Humphries
Send for Sidney. A Family Comedy
New York: Samuel French, 1940

Michael Jackson
Worksop of Yesterday
Worksop: Worksop Local History Society, 1969

M. Jagger
The History of Honley and Its Hamlets
Huddersfield: Alfred Jubb, 1914

C. James
Diseases Commonly Met with in Melanesia and Polynesia
Auckland: Institute Printing and Publishing Society, 1956 (4th edition)

Jesse James
Early United States Barbed Wire Patents
Maywood, Calif.: n.p., 1966

Dr Jekyll
A Sermon Preach'd at St-Mary-le-Bow, June 27 1698, before the
Societies for Reformation of Manners
Printed by R. & T. Mead for Ralph Simpson and Richard Cumberland, 1698

Tom Jones
A Catalogue of the Extremely Curious Valuable and Extensive
Musical Library Late the Property of T. Jones; also Copies of Mr
Jones's Music for the Harp
W. Watson, 1826

B. Lake
Knowledge for War: Every Officer's Handbook for the Front
Harrison & Sons, 1916

John Lennon
Low Temperature Ceramic Eutectic Glasses
Columbus, Ohio: Ohio State University, 1940

R. Maxwell
Borstal and Better. A Life Story
Hollis & Carter, 1956

Ian McGregor
Fundamental Techniques of Plastic Surgery
Edinburgh: Livingstone, 1960

SCHOOL EXPERIENCES

OF A FAG

AT A

PRIVATE AND A PUBLIC SCHOOL.

BY

GEORGE MELLY.

The possible early inspiration for the latter- day George Melly's candid autobiography, Rum, Bum and Concertina.

George Melly
School Experiences of a Fag at a Private and a Public School
Smith, Elder, 1854

John Milton
On Spermatorrhoea and Its Complications
H. Renshaw, 1881 (11th edition)

A History of Syphilis
Harrison & Sons, 1880

The Successful Treatment of Leprosy
Chatto & Windus, 1890

Frank Muir
Property and Income Tax Tables. By a Surveyor of Taxes
Blackwoods, 1860

Robert Redford
Apostolic Christianity and Other Sermons
Hodder & Stoughton, 1869

Jimmy Saville
An Essay on the Tendency of Mental Cultivation in Science and
Religion to Promote the Improvement of the Working Classes
n.p., 1850

15

David Steel
The Elements and Practice of Rigging and Seamanship
Printed for The Author, 1794

Elizabeth Taylor
Meditations of an Old Maid
Cincinnati, Ohio: n.p., c. 1900

Harold Wilson
The History and Significance of the Lord's Day
Christian Knowledge Society, 1910

Not Ian Fleming and Not the Princess of Wales

Anon. (definitely not Ian Fleming)
On Her Majesty's Secret Service
I. & R. Maxwell, 1878

Annette M. Lyster
The Ups and Downs of Lady Di
National Society's Depository, 1907

A Trio of Unlikely Thatchers

John Wells Thatcher*
Called to the Bar. A Story of the Middle Temple
Pitman, 1914

Pitman's Guide to the Law of Licensing. The Handbook for All
Licence-holders
Pitman, 1912
(*John Wells is a comic actor who impersonates Denis Thatcher, husband of
Margaret Thatcher.**)
(**Margaret Thatcher is a well-known British Prime Minister.)

M. Thatcher
Isis. A Divine Poem
J. Handyside, 1854 (25 copies only)

The cover picture of this unusually prophetic fairy story, published in 1907, depicts the moment when, although chaperoned, Lady Di's bustle is fondled by the old crone – who later turns into a handsome prince and marries her.

17

Miss Thatcher as featured in
Mad About Women
N. Reynold Packard
Obelisk Press, 1933

❛"Well, who's winning?" asked a feminine voice from behind us.

"My wife must still be true to me," said the fat one. "I haven't won a shake tonight."

"I'm sorry I don't know your name," the thin man apologized, turning to me.

I told him.

"Meet Miss Thatcher."

After another round of drinks, I found myself dancing with Miss Thatcher. She was a woman of between forty and fifty, with hair that was becoming gray and a face that was beginning to wrinkle. She had four or five moles sprinkled on her left cheek.

"You are very fascinating," I whispered in her ear as we danced.

"Don't talk silly. I'm old enough to be your mother."

"That is one of the reasons why I like you. I hate young girls."

"But young girls are lovely."

"At the most, only physically so. Please don't be mean to me just because I am younger than you. I really could love you if you would be kind to me and let my head rest on your breast. I know your breasts are lovely like two soft pigeons."

"You are drunk, that's all. You don't mean what you say."

"Yes, I do. If you will see me tomorrow night I'll prove it."

"Will you be sober?"

"Not unless you insist on it."

"I certainly do. I must take you in hand, little boy."

"I like that. Little boy! Still, if you would mother me I wouldn't mind. But what about tomorrow?"

"It's no use. I can't start playing around with boys at my age."

"But I'm not a bottle of wine that has to be old before it's any good. You might at least give me a try."

"What shall we do tomorrow if I do meet you?"

"Go to supper, the theatre, and then, if everything goes well, you might invite me in. That is, if you can. . . ."

Our bodies bumped together and I no longer heard the popping of the coals nor saw the phantasmagoria on the walls. In the stillness that came afterward, I thought of the softness, almost flabbiness, of her breasts. They seemed more soothing, more desirable than the hard, antagonistic protuberances of Mary Bella and Anita.

"That was lovely," I said to her as I left that night.❜

3
Names to Conjure With
Extraordinary authors' names

"There's nowt so queer as folk", as the old saying goes; and there's nowt queerer about them than some of their names. We give you our word of honour that all the following are hundred-per-cent-genuine names of real authors – or, at least, authors (and, in a few instances, the subjects of biographies) under whose names books are listed in the catalogues of the British Library and in the American National Union Catalog.

There is an appalling greed that grips writers like us in quest of the bizarre. Not content with unearthing these poor souls from their catalogue graves, we want more. We want Don Bolognese and Camillo Ravioli to have written an Italian cookery book; Apathy and Banal to team up as the dullest co-authors ever. We want to know if Kersi D. Doodha was the brother (or sister?) of Zipper D. Doodha, and whether Eugeniusz Dalek and Walter Womble ever considered appearing in children's television programmes. Did Lunge and Hurter belong to the same club? Did Gergely Gergely's parents have a warped sense of humour? Did O. Heck ever meet O. Hell? Did Mrs Bleeker Bangs get fed up with smutty jokes about her name? And as Urban Grosskipper von Wipper is a pseudonym, whatever was his *real* name?

Istvan Apathy
Gaspar Griswold Bacon
Pierre Jean Jacques
    Bacon-Tacon
Nellie Badcock
Ole Bagger
Marmaduke Baglehole
Ludwig von Baldass
Melville Balsillie[1]
Jean Baptiste Banal
Ole Bang[2]
Rebecca Hammering Bang
Mrs Bleeker Bangs
Marmaduke Bannister
Ida Barney
Virgil L. Bedsole[3]
Krista Bendová[4]
Arngrim Berserk[5]

Myrtle Berry
Nicolas Bidet
John Thomas Bigge
Juana Bignozzi
René Palaprat de Bigot
Petr Bitsilli
Balthasar Blutfogel
Mody Coggin Boatright[6]
Don Bolognese
Hugo Bonk
Kah-Ge-Ga-Gah-Bowh[7]
Wallop Brabazon
William Brassier
Melt Brink
Malte Brunk
Knud Bugge
Al Burt
Caspar Bussing

Perin H. Cabinetmaker
Desiré Carnel
Emu Ceka[8]
Jacob Grubbe Cock
Paul Condom
Ellsworth Prouty Conkle[9]
Ettrick Creak
Clement Crock
Lettice May Crump
Eugeniusz Dalek
Dee Day
T. Fox Decent
Mahew Derryberry
Roger A. Destroyer
Robert Baby Buntin Dicebat[10]
Arsen Diklić
Kersi D. Doodha
Ebenezer (5) Duty of Ohio[11]
Gottfried Egg
Bernt Eggen
Ekkehard Eggs
Gordon Bandy Enders
Jacob Fagot
Achilles Fang
Vera Fartash
A. Farto
Francis M. Fillerup
Gottfried Finger
Stuyvesant Fish
Hans Flasche
Mercedes Fórmica
Semen Frug
Stanka Fuckar
Gergely Gergely
Biserka Grabar
Roland Grassberger
George L. Grassmuck
Jānis Grots

Grub-dbang bKrashis
 rGyal-mtshan
 Dri-med sNying-po
Billings Learned Hand
Odd Bang Hansen
O. Heck
O. Hell
Burt Heywang[12]
J. Hogsflesh
Frederik Winkel Horn
Albert Irk
Jup Kastrati
Solon Toothaker Kimball
Kurt Kink
A. Kipper
Onno Klopp
Hieronimus Knicker
Johannes Kurzwelly
Dirk La Cock
George Lunge[13]
Manfred Lurker
Ross Mangles
Voltaire Molesworth
Professor A. Moron
Lucretia Coffin Mott
Rocco L. Motto
John Muckarsie
Violet Organ
Alfra B. Pant
Rene Perve
Willy Prick
Willibald Psychyrembel
Ruth Rice Puffer
Mme J. J. Fouqueau de Pussy
Willem Quackelbeen
Camillo Ravioli
Hans Rectanus
Curt Redslob

Valve Ristok
A. Rump
A. Schytte
James Patrick Sex
Isac Shag
I. I. Shitts
Mrs Hepsa Ely Silliman
Ivor Snook

Negley King Teeters
Morten Thing
Anna Ethel Twitt De Vere[14]
Urban Grosskipper von
   Wipper[15]
Walter Womble
Ole Worm
Sabina Wurmbrand

1. Author of *Let's Enjoy Ourselves* (The Cadet Supply Association, 1960).
2. Author of *Rotterne* (Copenhagen: Gyldendalske Boghandel, 1936).
3. Co-author of the celebrated *A History of Western Civilization* (Baton Rouge, La.: Louisiana State University Press, 1936).
4. Author of *Čačky-hračky* (Bratislava: Mladé Letá, 1958).
5. Pseudonym of Olof Von Dalin.
6. Co-author, with James F. Dobie, of *Straight Texas* (Austin, Tex.: Folk Lore Society of Texas, 1937).
7. Later changed his name to George Copway.
8. Pseudonym. His real name was F. Muck.
9. Author of *Crick Bottom Plays* (1928), *Poor Old Bongo* (1954), and *Son-of-a-Biscuit-Eater* (1958), all published in New York by Samuel French.
10. His collected poems were published under the title *Superman* (Constable, 1934).
11. The "(5)" appears as part of his name in the British Library catalogue.
12. Author of *Poultry Management in Subtropical, Semiarid Climates* (Washington, DC: United States Department of Agriculture, 1937).
13. Co-author with Ferdinand Hurter.
14. Inventor of shorthand system.
15. Pseudonym.

GASPAR GRISWOLD BACON

4
The Right Person for the Job
Authors whose names are remarkably appropriate – or totally inappropriate – to the subjects of their books

There is a long literary tradition that derives humour from people's names being appropriate to their personalities. On a lower level, everyone is familiar with examples of names that relate closely to jobs – "I. Pullem, Dentist", that sort of thing. Less well documented are those authors whose names seem tailor-made for the subjects of their books – though in some instances, the tailor seems to have got the measurements wrong.

One might pause to speculate on how such coincidences of name and title come about. Did James Bent somehow feel compelled by an irresistible fate to become a police officer and then to write about his experiences – thus becoming the ultimate "bent copper"? Did Mr Battie have to write on madness and Frank Finn on aquaria? Didn't anyone notice that Adrienne Swindells was not exactly the most appropriate name for the author of a book on crime? Or is there perhaps a slight suggestion that titles are occasionally contrived to fit their author's name: Elbow's *Writing with Power* and the phrase "more power to your elbow" feel just too "right". Some names, indeed, turn out to be pseudonyms chosen, one feels certain, for their obvious link with the subject matter – for example, Tom Rodway, the author of *Teach Yourself Fishing* (English Universities Press, 1950), was really one Richard Luis Owen Waddington. However, in our select list of names that fit – or don't, as the case may be – we have attempted to include only those we believe to be fortuitous rather than fabricated.

The Cypress Garden
Jane Arbor
Mills & Boon, 1969

The Politics of Weapons Innovation
Michael Armacost
New York and London: Columbia University Press, 1969

Punishment
Robin Banks
Harmondsworth: Penguin, 1972

Art of Editing
Floyd K. Baskette and Jack Z. Sissors
West Drayton: Collier Macmillan, 1982

A

TREATISE

ON

MADNESS.

By WILLIAM BATTIE M. D.

Fellow of the College of Phyſicians in LONDON,

And Phyſician to St. Luke's Hoſpital.

LONDON;

Printed for J. WHISTON, and B. WHITE, in Fleet-ſtreet.

M,DCC,LVIII.

[Price Two Shillings and Six-Pence.]

"Battie's the name, lunacy's the game...."

CRIMINAL LIFE:

REMINISCENCES

OF

FORTY-TWO YEARS AS A POLICE OFFICER.

BY

SUPERINTENDENT BENT.

—

JOHN HEYWOOD,
DEANSGATE AND RIDGEFIELD, MANCHESTER;
1, PATERNOSTER BUILDINGS,
LONDON.

ENTERED AT STATIONER'S HALL.

*"Anything you say
will be taken down…*

*…and may be used in
my autobiography."*

Criminal Life: Reminiscences of Forty-Two Years as a Police Officer
Superintendent James Bent
Manchester: John Heywood, 1891

Cavities and Waveguides with Inhomogeneous and Anisotropic Media
A. Berk
Cambridge, Mass.: The MIT Press, 1955

Les Classes Dirigeantes*
Charles Bigot
Paris: Charpentier et Cie, 1875
[*The Ruling Classes]

Farm Poultry Raising
Herbert Roderick Bird
Washington, DC: United States Department of Agriculture, 1948

Alpine Plants of Distinction
A. Bloom
Collingridge, 1968

Diseases of the Nervous System
Walter Russell Brain (Baron Brain)
Oxford: Oxford University Press, 1933

Home Wine-making
Harold Edwin Bravery
New York: Arco Publishing Co., 1968

Handbuch der Massage
Anton Bum
Berlin: Urban & Schwarzenberg, 1907

The Inner Flame
Clara Louise Burnham
Constable, 1912

Discovering Bells and Bellringing
John Camp
Tring: Shire Publications, 1968

Motorcycling for Beginners
Geoff Carless
East Ardsley: EP Publishing, 1980

La Libertine
Nonce Casanova
Amiens: E. Malfère, 1921

The Abel Coincidence
J. N. Chance
Robert Hale, 1969

The Preacher; or, The Art and Method of Preaching
W. Chappell
Edward Farnham, 1656

Your Teeth
John Chipping
Cottrell & Co., 1967

Oppositions of Religious Doctrines
William A. Christian
Macmillan, 1972

A Botanic Guide to Health
Albert Isaiah Coffin
Leeds: Moxon, 1845

Predicting the Child's Development
W. F. Dearborn
Cambridge, Mass.: Sci-Art Publishers, 1941

Inside Story
A. Dick
Allen & Unwin, 1943

Violence Against Wives
Emerson and Russell Dobash
Shepton Mallet: Open Books, 1980

Textile Fabrics
Elizabeth Dyer
Boston: Houghton Mifflin, 1923

Writing with Power
Peter Elbow
Oxford: Oxford University Press, 1981

How to Live to a Hundred Years or More
George Fasting
New York: The Author, 1927

Causes of Crime
A. Fink
Philadelphia, Pa.: University of Pennsylvania Press, 1938

26

The Boy's Own Aquarium
Frank Finn
Country Life and George Newnes, 1922

A Bibliography of Water Pollution and Its Control
Hugh Fish
Henley-on-Thames: Gothard House, 1972

Sewage Treatment and Disposal
G. M. Flood
Blackie, 1926

Round the Bend in the Stream
Sir Wilmot Hudson Fysh
Sydney and London: Angus & Robertson, 1968

Common Truths from Queer Texts
Revd Joseph Gay
Arthur Stockwell, 1908

The Bog People
P. V. Glob
Faber & Faber, 1969

The Encyclopaedia of Association Football
Maurice Golesworthy
Robert Hale, 1967

Illustrated History of Gymnastics
John Goodbody
Stanley Paul, 1983

Running Duck
Paula Gosling
Pan Books, 1979

Discovering Horn
Paula Hardwick
Lutterworth, 1981

Handbook of Trees, Shrubs and Roses
Walter Gordon Hazlewood
Sydney and London: Angus & Robertson, 1968 (2nd edition)

The High Rise
Leo Heaps
W. H. Allen, 1972

Chess Pieces
Norman Knight
Sutton Coldfield: Chess, 1968

International Dairy Situation and Outlook
W. Krostitz (of "The Milk and Milk Products Team")
Rome: FAO, 1976

The Home Book of Turkish Cookery
Venice Lamb
Faber & Faber, 1969

Reproduction in the Female Mammal
George Eric Lamming and Emmanuel Cipriano Amoroso (eds.)
Butterworth, 1968

Psychological Warfare
P. M. A. Linebarger
Washington, DC: Infantry Journal Press, 1948

Of Such Is the Kingdom: a Nativity Play
Gladys Littlechild
Methuen, 1952

Anatomy of the Brain
William W. Looney
Philadelphia, Pa.: F. A. Davis, 1932 (2nd edition)

Grace of God
A. Lord
Truro: James R. Netherton, 1859

Crocheting Novelty Pot-holders
L. Macho
New York: Dover, 1982

When I Was a Boy; or, She Touched the Right Chord
Maria Manley
William Macintosh, 1864

Riches and Poverty
L. G. Chiozza Money
Methuen, 1905

The Lord's Supper
William Gilbert Ovens
Church Association, 1940

Spices from the Lord's Garden
Revd E. I. D. Pepper
West Conshohocken, Pa.: n.p., 1895

Land Speed Record. A Complete History of the Record-breaking Cars from 39 to 600+ mph
Cyril Posthumus
Reading: Osprey, 1971

Nutrition and Diet Therapy
Fairfax Throckmorton Proudfit
New York: Macmillan, 1938 (7th edition)

The Trimming and Finishing of Hosiery and Hosiery Fabrics
J. H. Quilter
Bradford: C. Greening, 1889

A-Saddle in the Wild West
William Henry Rideing
J. C. Nimmo, 1879

The Professionals: Prostitutes and Their Clients
Iain Scarlet
Sidgwick & Jackson, 1972

The Doctor's Case Against the Pill
Barbara Seaman
New York: P. H. Wyman, 1969; Michael Joseph, 1970

By Reef and Shoal
William Sinker
Christian Knowledge Society, 1904

The Skipper's Secret
Robert Smellie
Edinburgh: D. M. Small, 1898

Price Expectations and the Behaviour of the Price Level
R. Solow
Manchester: Manchester University Press, 1970

Electronics for Schools
R. A. Sparkes
Hutchinson Educational, 1972

Crime and Law
Adrienne P. Swindells*
Hart-Davis, 1977
(*Also author of *Running a Disco, Drugs* and *Throwing a Party*
(Hart-Davis, 1978).)

The Imperial Animal
Lionel Tiger and Robin Fox
Secker & Warburg, 1972

La Formation de la Jeunesse
Désiré Tits
Brussels: Office de Publicité, 1945

Operation Earth
B. Trench
Neville Spearman, 1969

The Eighth Passenger
Miles Tripp
Heinemann, 1969

There Are No Problem Horses, Only Problem Riders
Mary Twelveponies
Boston, Mass.: Houghton Mifflin, 1982

Rope
William Tyson
Wheatland Journals, 1968

Fuel Oil Viscosity-Temperature Diagram
Guysbert B. Vroom
New York and London: Simmons-Boardman, 1926

Underground Jerusalem
Sir Charles Warren
R. Bentley & Son, 1876

The Principles of Insect Philosophy
V. B. Wigglesworth
Methuen, 1939

The World of My Books
I. M. Wise
Cincinnati, Ohio: American Jewish Archives, 1954

Spine Titles

The convention of abbreviating authors' names and titles to make them fit on the spine of a book, and the use of the formula "surname + on + subject" sometimes produces unfortunate results:

Ball on the Rectum
Sir Charles Bent Ball, *The Rectum*
(Hodder & Stoughton, 1908)

Gotobed on Darts
Jabez Gotobed, *Darts: Fifty Ways to Play the Game*
(Cambridge: Oleander, 1980)

Hogg on Sheep
James Hogg, *The Shepherd's Guide: Being a Practical Treatise on the Diseases of Sheep*
(Edinburgh: Archibald Constable, 1807)

Miles on the Horse's Foot
William Miles, *The Horse's Foot*
(Longman, 1846)

Tredd on Dice
William Evan Tredd, *Dice Games New & Old*
(Cambridge: Oleander, 1981)

Watts on the Mind
Isaac Watts, *The Improvement of the Mind*
(Printed for J. Brackstone, 1741)

Withering's Botany
William Withering, *A Botanical Arrangement of British Plants*
(Birmingham: Printed by M. Swinney, 1776)

5
A Musical Interlude
Suggestions for an offbeat soirée

This impressive selection of sheet-music titles from the British Library's vast collection has been made with an eye to the growing revival of the Victorian musical evening. However, it is suggested that the children are tucked up in bed first, for some of the lyrics cannot, with propriety, be sung by junior members of the family.

Art' Coming?
Leo Kerbusch, 1860
The song begins, "Deeper and deeper".

Aspirations of Youth
Marcus Hast, 1874
The song begins, "Higher, Higher".

Ballads for Babies, with Merry Movements
Jennett Humphreys, 1888

Ball Tossing
H. Lottner, 1894

Beware my Fanny
John S. Geldard, c. 1820
"Behold! my Fanny, yonder flow'r
How droops its lovely head –
It blows, and yet another hour
It withers and is dead."

The Blind Boy
C. Cibber, 1874
The song begins, "Oh! say what is that thing?"

The Blind Boy
Kate Fanny Loder, 1873
The song begins, "I feel with delight".

Both Old Men and Young; or, The Well Dispos'd Organ Blower
Anon., c. 1730

Camping
Alec Rowley, 1928
In the *When I'm a Man* series.

Come Before Mother Is Up
Edward Cympson (pseudonym of E. Sibson), 1876

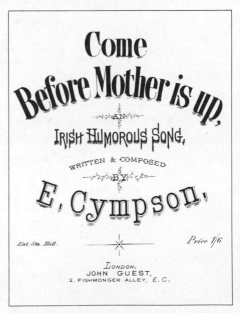

Edward Cympson's irresistible musical invitation to dawn dalliance in Erin while mother has a lie-in.

Dance of the Rubber Dolls
Paul La Valle, 1919

The Faggot-binders' Chorus
Anon., n.d.

Fair Cloris in a Pigstye Lay
"By a Welch Gentleman", c. 1720

Fairy-Fingered Fanny
Alfred E. Aarons, n.d.

The Fairy's Ball
Edith Dick, 1924

Fixed in His Everlasting Seat
Georg Friedrich Haendel, 1899

A Frenchman's Letter to His English Mistress
Anon., 1752

Galloping Dick
Percy Fletcher and G. Rothery, 1911

Gay Go Up
R. H. Walther, n.d.

The Gay Photographer
G. Grossmith, n.d.

A Handy Little Thing to Have About You
Harold Montague, n.d.

Hard at First; or, I'm a Daddy At It Now
Norton Atkins, 1894

Hörst der Erste Laut
Josef Licharz, 1957

I'd Tell You if I Were a Little Fly
Augustus Leach, 1877

I'll Place It in the Hands of My Solicitor
F. Gilbert, 1887

I Love Little Pussy
H. Farmer, n.d.

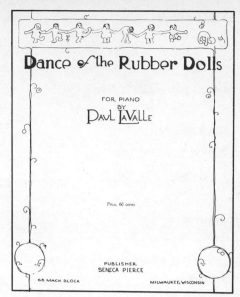

The title-page of a bouncy little number.

I Love Little Willie
John Jacob Niles, 1955
"To be sung in a gay, mocking manner".

I Love My Love in the Morning
J. K. D. Bedwell, n.d.

I'm a Very Potent Queen
Georg Jacobi and L. H. F. de Terreaux, 1873

In the Depths of the Sea
T. T. Peed, n.d.

In Vain I Strive with Aspect Gay; or, Up All Night
Matthew Peter King, n.d.

I Smote Him on the Boko with My Whangee
William Hyde, n.d.

It's Really Quite Hard
Anon., 1899
The song begins, "It's apt to be embarrassing".

I Was Holding My Cocoanut
Charles Collins and J. Burley, n.d.

Let Us Be Gay
George Linley, c. *1835*
"A favourite song in the musical drama of *The Queen and the Cardinal*".

I Wasn't a Bit Like a Boy
E. Solomon, *n.d.*

I Won't Be a Nun
Countess W-N-K, *n.d.*

The Joy-inspiring Horn
R. Bride, *n.d.*

Kornblumen
F. Arter, *1854*

A Large Cold Bottle and a Small Hot Bird
John A. Stromberg, *1898*

The Lapful of Nuts
Alicia Adelaide Needham, *1914*

Let Me Hold It Till I Die
H. Lovegrove, *1864*

Loo Galop and Loo Waltz
J. Frascati, *1875*
"Played nightly at the Strand Theatre".

Love and a Bumper; or, Fanny's Delight; or, Come Sweet Lass
Anon., c. *1750*

The Man with the Four Point Seven!
Gaston de Breville, *1912*

The Medical Wife
"F.I.", *1871*
The song begins, "I'm the queerest of husbands".

Miniwanka; or, The Moments of the Water
Robert M. Schafer, *1973*

The Monks Were Jolly Boys
From the operetta *Once Too Often* by Howard Glover, *1862*

The Mumps
Mana Zuccer, *1934*

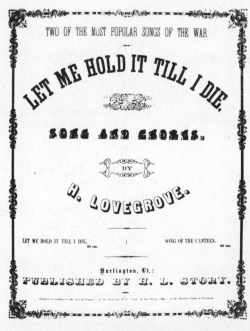

An unusual last request in Mr Lovegrove's song of the American Civil War.

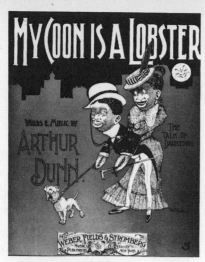

A bizarre song about race relations among crustaceans.

My Coon is a Lobster
Arthur Dunn, 1899
"Ev'ry body says that you are a lobster,
Tell me what that is right away.
He said a lobster is a man who never
    has a cent
And takes all the money from his wife.

Then I told him to his face
If that is the case
He's been a lobster all his life.
Then his face turned white,
First time in his life."

My Nancy Loves Me Truly. An Agricultural Lay
W. Yardley, 1883

The Nobility Balls Polka
Anon., 1844
"With military band parts".

No More Fancy Balls for Me
N. Atkins and Herbert Darnley, n.d.
"No more fancy balls for me!
They suit the aristocracy and parsons;
But if I have to go to any more balls
It'll be the old three brass 'uns."

Open Thy Lattice, Darling!
G. H. Newcombe, 1890

Saw Ye My Wee Thing?
Anon., c. 1796

Say Mamma, If He Pops Shall I Send Him to You?
Henry S. Leigh, 1874

A Sea Side Lay
C. L. Kenney, 1882

The Snail's Galop
E. de Gremont, 1867

Sweet Dangle, Pride of Erin
E. Ransford, 1870

They've All Got Sticky Backs
J. W. Knowles, 1903

Uncle John, the Lay of the Hopeful Nephew
Henry S. Leigh, 1870

Wanderin' Willie; or, Here Awa', There Awa'
W. Moodie, 1902

When War's Alarms Entic'd My Willy from Me
T. Linley, c. 1770

With My Little Wigger-wagger in My Hand
F. Earle, Frank Carter and Gilbert Wells, 1909

Ye Nymphs of Bath Prepare the Lay; or, On Princess Amelia
Maurice Greene, 1737

Yielding Fanny
Anon., c. 1750

You Do Keep Popping In and Out
Albert Hall and J. W. Knowles, 1904

The Young Nun
Augusto Rotoli, 1884
The song begins "When from above I seek relief".

You're Getting It Up for Me
Augustus Leach, 1878

6
We Have a Book On It
Astonishingly specialized subjects

The story is told of a little girl who borrowed from her public library Dr Bernard Stonehouse's definitive book on king penguins (the birds, that is, not the books). When she returned it, the librarian enquired whether she had enjoyed it. "This book told me more than I ever wanted to know about penguins", was her doleful and memorable reply.

The books that follow have been selected for their remarkable narrowness of specialization. While we acknowledge that if, for example, you are passionate about Chinese footbinding, truncheons or crumhorns, you may well find among them the book you have always been looking for, there is rather more likelihood that you will sympathize with our young student of penguins.

The Human Factor in Game–Vehicle Accidents. A Study of Drivers' Information Acquisition
Lars Aberg
Stockholm: Almqvist & Wiksell, 1981

'The general purpose of the present study is to study different aspects of human behaviour in relation to game–vehicle accidents in general. The study has been confined to accidents involving moose, mainly because the consequencies [*sic*] in general are more serious than those of other wildlife accidents.' (Publisher's catalogue.)

Millennium Charisma Among the Pathans
Akbar S. Ahmed
Routledge & Kegan Paul, 1976

The Care of Raw Hide Drop Box Loom Pickers
Anon.
Saco, Me.: Garland Manufacturing Co., 1922

How to Prepare and Run a Simple T.E.W.T.*
Anon.
Aldershot: Gale & Polden, 1943
[*Tactical Exercise Without Troops]

Octogenarian Teetotalers, with One Hundred and Thirteen Portraits
Anon.
National Temperance League Publication Depot, 1897
First the "Unique Reception" in the Town Hall of St Martin-in-the-Fields on 21 May 1896, and now the book!

Probably the only illustrated directory of geriatric abstainers ever published, it was not a bestseller – more a dire warning.

Le Pénis et la Démoralisation de l'Occident
Jean Paul Aron
Paris: Bernard Grasset, 1978

Why People Move
Jorge Balan (ed.)
Paris: UNESCO, 1981

English Picnics
Esther Georgina Battiscombe
Harvill Press, 1949

Der Begriff 'Silly Fool' im Slang einer englischen Schule
H. Beck
Bern: Francke Verlag, 1982

The Development of a Procedure for Eliciting Information from Boys about the Nature and Extent of Their Stealing
William Albert Belson, G. L. Millerson and P. J. Didcott
London School of Economics, n.d.

The Unconscious Significance of Hair
George Charles Berg
George Allen & Unwin, 1951

Organizing Deviance
Joel Best and David F. Luckenbill
Englewood Cliffs, NJ: Prentice-Hall, 1982

Shoe Bottom Costing
E. S. Bream
The British Boot, Shoe and Allied Trades Research Association, 1936

The Classification of Mankind by the Hair and Wool of Their Head
with an Answer to Dr Prichard's Assertion, that "The Covering of the Head of the Negro Is Hair, Properly So Termed and Not Wool"
Peter Arrell Browne
Philadelphia, Pa.: n.p., 1850

A Glowing and Graphic Description of the Great Hole
Mrs D.U.C.
Syracuse, NY: Daily Democrat Office, 1848

Hours of Love
R. Carrera
Lausanne: Scriptor, c. 1978
On "erotic watches".

Timber-Framed Buildings in Watford
S. A. Castle
Chichester: Phillimore, 1977

Jaws and Teeth of Ancient Hawaiians
H. G. Chappel
Honolulu: Honolulu Museum, 1927

The History of the Self-winding Watch, 1770–1931
Alfred Chapuis and Eugène Jaquet
Neuchâtel: Editions du Griffon, 1952; Batsford (trans. Renée Savarè Grandvoinet), 1952

Faith, Reason and The Plague in Seventeenth Century Tuscany
Carlo Cipolla
Hassocks: Harvester Press, 1979

Truncheons: Their Romance and Reality
Erland Fenn Clark
Herbert Jenkins, 1935
With over 100 plates illustrating more than 500 truncheons.

The Rhinoceros in Art: from Dürer to Stubbs
T. H. Clark
Philip Wilson Publishers, "forthcoming"

Wall-Paintings by Snake Charmers in Tanganyika
Hans Cory
Faber & Faber, 1953

Paintings and Drawings on the Backs of National Gallery Pictures
Martin Davies
National Gallery, 1946

Like the B-side of a record, the flip side of a picture is frequently more interesting than the better-known masterpiece, and this book gives us a unique opportunity to view some choice examples. Here, for instance, instead of a rather dull portrait of Savonarola, we are introduced to the picture on the back – the burning of Savonarola, Domenico da Pescia and Silvestro Maruffi in the Piazza della Signora, Florence, on 23 May 1498 – a spirited scene depicting the three malefactors being well toasted, with eager helpers rushing to the blaze with bundles of faggots. This revelatory book prompts one to enquire just what lurks on the backs of some other famous paintings? A sketch of Mona Lisa scowling? An obscene drawing of a farm wench on the reverse of Constable's *Hay Wain*?

Moles and Their Meaning.
With Regard to the Mind, Morals and Astral Indications in Both Sexes, Being a Modernised and Easy Guide to the Ancient Science of Divination by the Moles of the Human Body (Founded on the Works and Researches of one Richard Sanders, A.D. 1653, and Other Eminent Astrologers of About the Same Period.)
Harry de Windt
C. Arthur Pearson, 1907
The definitive work on moleosophy.

Despite the facial microdot, this is not an insight into the motives of spies, but a detailed investigation of the technique of "reading" a person's character from their bodily blemishes – a rather specialized branch of the pseudo-science of anthroposcopy.

Male Infibulation
Eric John Dingwall
John Bale, Sons & Danielsson (Studies in the Sexual Lives of Ancient and Mediaeval Peoples, Vol. 1), 1925

An Objective Study of Punctuality in Relation to Personality and Achievement
George John Dudycha
New York: Archives of Psychology, 1936

The Social History of the Machine Gun
John Ellis
New York: Pantheon Books, 1975

Camel Brands and Graffiti from Iraq, Syria, Jordan, Iran and Arabia
Henry Field
Baltimore, Md.: American Oriental Association, 1952

Skeletal Remains of the Central Eskimos
Knud Ejvind Fischer-Møller
Copenhagen: Gyldendalske Boghandel, 1937

Also and Too: a Corpus-based Study of Their Frequency and Use in Modern English
B. Fjelkestam-Nilsson
Stockholm: Almqvist & Wiksell, 1983

The Inheritance of Hairy Ear Rims
Reginald Ruggles Gates and P. N. Bhaduri
Edinburgh: Mankind Quarterly, n.d.

The Cambridgeshire Coprolite Mining Rush
Richard Grove
Cambridge: Oleander, 1976

The Loathsomeness of Long Haire . . .
with the Concurrent Judgement of Divines Both Old and New Against It. With an Appendix Against Painting, Spots, Naked Breasts, etc.
Revd Thomas Hall
n.p., 1654

Philippe Halsman's Jump Book
Philippe Halsman
André Deutsch, 1959

‘This book shows 178 jumps executed by some of the most prominent and important people of our society: political figures, leaders of industry, famous scientists, artists and writers, Nobel Prize winners, judges, theologians, movie stars, TV performers and outstanding athletes.’

For several years, whenever the late Philippe Halsman received an assignment to photograph anyone famous, he asked them if they would also pose for him jumping in the air. Some, including Lord Mountbatten and Bertrand Russell, refused. Dame Edith Evans could hardly walk, so he decided not to ask her to attempt a leap. But plenty of other people agreed, and this extraordinary book is the result.

In his introduction, Halsman discusses "Symbolism in Jumping" and the importance of the positions of the arms and legs. His photograph of Dali jumping, with an arc of water and flying cats, is appropriately surrealistic and has become a classic; with most of the others, one is left with a feeling of wonderment not only at Halsman's reasons for compiling such a weird book, but also as to why many more "prominent and important people" (such as Edith Sitwell, who described him as "a horrid little man") didn't simply tell him to bugger off.

"The Pogo Prince and the Amazing Flying Wallis": The Duke and Duchess of Windsor pose in mid-leap for the camera of Philippe Halsman. The Duke is wearing his special Prince-of-Wales-check jumpsuit.

41

The Problem of Nonsense Linguistics
Goran Hammarstrom
Stockholm: Almqvist & Wiksell, 1971

The 'Walking Stick' Method of Self-Defence
Herbert Gordon Lang
Athletic Publications, 1926
Basically a manual illustrating numerous ways of whacking someone with a stick. It contains chapters with such evocative titles as "'Flicks' and 'Flips'", "Cuts" and "Active Stick Play", and fifty-nine lively photographs.

Chinese Footbinding. The History of a Curious Erotic Custom
Howard Seymour Levy
Neville Spearman, 1970

A Toddler's Guide to the Rubber Industry
D. Lowe
Leicester: De Montfort Press, 1947
A reissue in book form of essays published in the *India-Rubber Review* employing an "Alice in Rubberland" framework.

As the *India-Rubber Journal* said of Mr Lowe's other book, *A Toddler's Guide to Big Business*, "The book is written in satirical vein, but it points a moral and in parts makes amusing reading."

Bead Making in Scandinavia in the Early Middle Ages
Agneta Lundström
Stockholm: Almqvist & Wiksell, 1976

The Causes of Poverty
Callaghan MacCarthy
P. S. King & Sons, 1908
The succinct reply might be, "not enough money". However, MacCarthy goes into rather more detail:

‘The people of the United Kingdom invest £264 million and spend £1,486 million – £575 million on the prevention of evil and unproductive consumption . . . in other words, the prevention of evil and unproductive consumption demand 575/1,486ths of the services annually used up.’

"Unproductive consumption" is defined by Mr MacCarthy as:

‘Excessive quantities or qualities of food, drink, clothing, furniture, heating and lighting, house decoration, housing, means of locomotion, gardens, parks, means of recreation, books, newspapers, literature generally, places of worship and religion, ceremonial requirements, articles of personal adornment, club premises, theatres, architectural display, public buildings, public monuments, artistic collections, travelling comforts, hunting, shooting, motoring, yachting, racing and sporting requirements; from unfinished materials, implements, machinery, factories, vegetable life, animal life, lands, quarries, mines and other items employed for the purpose of producing the property referred to in this paragraph; and finally from shops, streets, roads, docks, quays, railways, tramways, rolling stock, telephones, telegraphs and other forms employed in its distribution. . . . we may form a vague notion as to the volume of services directed from property towards the gratification of human desires, and that, ultimately, fails to add anything to human growth. '

Anglo-Saxon Writs
Florence Elizabeth Harmer
Manchester: Manchester University Press, 1952

The Music of the Mongols
Reports from the Sven Hedin Sino-Swedish Expedition
Stockholm: Almqvist & Wiksell, 1943

Short-term Visual Information Forgetting
A. H. C. Van Der Heijden
International Library of Psychology and Routledge, 1981

Locomotive Boiler Explosions
Christian H. Hewison
Newton Abbot: David & Charles, 1983
"Always engrossing . . . sometimes disturbing". (Book club advertisement.)

The Madam as Entrepreneur: Career Management in House Prostitution
Barbara Sherman Heyl
New Brunswick, NJ: Transaction Books, 1978

Red-White-Black as a Mode of Thought.
A Study of Triadic Classification by Colours in the Ritual Symbolism and Cognitive Thought of the Peoples of the Lower Congo
A. Jacobson-Widing
Stockholm: Almqvist & Wiksell, 1979

Greek Pins and Their Connexions with Europe and Asia
Paul Jacobsthal
Oxford: Oxford University Press, 1956

Oh Angry Sea (a-ab-ba, hu-luh-ha): the History of a Sumerian Congregational Lament
Raphael Kutscher
New Haven, Conn.: Yale University Press, 1975

Fish-Hooks in Africa and Their Distribution
Sture Lagercrantz
Stockholm: Statens Etnografiska Museum, 1934
Mr Lagercrantz then turned his attention to:

Penis Sheaths and Their Distribution in Africa
Uppsala: Uppsala University, 1976

43

The Railways of Tottenham
G. H. Lake
Greenlake Publications, 1945

Hints to Paviors
Col. Francis Maceroni*
Knight & Lacy, 1827
(*Aide-de-camp* to Joachim Murat, King of Naples.)

How to Fill Mental Cavities
Bill Maltz
Beverly Hills, Calif.: Marlbro, 1978

Wall-to-Wall America: a Cultural History of Post-Office Murals in the Great Depression
Karal Ann Marling
Minneapolis, Minn.: University of Minnesota Press, 1982

Fifty New Creative Poodle Grooming Styles
Faye Meadows
New York: Arco Publishing Co., 1981

Oedipus in the Trobriands
E. Spiro Melford
Chicago, Ill.: University of Chicago Press, 1982

Manhole Covers of Los Angeles
Robert and Mimi Melnick
Los Angeles, Calif.: Dawson's Book Shop, 1974

The Crumhorn: Its History, Design, Repertory and Technique
Kenton Terry Meyer
Ann Arbor, Mich.: UMI Research, 1983

Simulacra
John Michell
Thames & Hudson, 1979
A book about things that look like other things.

Nature and Language: a Semiotic Study of Cucurbits in Literature
Ralf Norrman and Jon Haarberg
Routledge & Kegan Paul, 1980

Child-spacing in Tropical Africa
Hilary J. Page and Ron Lesthaege (eds.)
Academic Press, 1981

A History of Orgies
Burgo Partridge
Anthony Blond, 1958

Steam on the Isle of Wight, 1956–1966
Peter and Ken Paye
Oxford: Oxford Railway Publishing Co., 1979

On the Skull and Portraits of George Buchanan
Karl Pearson
Edinburgh: Oliver & Boyd, 1926
And also:

The Skull and Portraits of Henry Stewart, Lord Darnley
Cambridge: Biometika, 1928

Defensive Tactics with Flashlights
John G. Peters, Jr
Northbrook, Ill.: Calibre Press, 1983

The Unlovelinesse of Love-Locks
William Prynne
n.p., 1628

The History and Romance of Elastic Webbing Since the Dawn of Time
Clifford A. Richmond
Easthampton, Mass.: Published by The Author, n.d.

Sturgeon Hooks of Eurasia
Geza de Rohan-Csermak
Chicago, Ill.: Aldine Publishing Co., 1963

The Androgynous Manager
Alice Sargent
New York: Amacom, 1980

The Gay Astrologer
John Savage
New York: Ashley Books, 1982

Movie Stars in Bathtubs
Jack Scagnetti
Middle Village, NY: Jonathan David Publishers, 1975

Violence as Communication
Alex Schmid and Janny De Graaf
Beverly Hills, Calif.: Sage Publications, 1982

Sherpa Architecture
Valerio Sestini and Enzo Somigli (trans. Timothy Paterson)
Paris: UNESCO, 1978

Hours and Earnings in the Leather-glove Industry
Rebecca Glover Smaltz
Washington, DC: United States Government Printing Office, 1934

From the Monotremes to the Madonna. A Study of the Breast in Culture and Religion
Fabius Zachary Snoop
John Bale, Sons & Danielsson, 1928

"The poet ... takes the universe to be only an overwhelming maternity ... perfecting the breast was Nature's supreme endeavour", as can be assessed in such chapters as:

The Fragrant Bosom of Aphrodite
The Bosom of the Father
Aaron's Breastplate
Mountains of Myrrh
The Bloody Teat
Vests

Palaeopathological and Palaeoepidemiological Study of Osseous Syphilis in the Skulls of the Edo Period
Takao Suzuki
Tokyo: University of Tokyo Press, 1984

The Pleasures of the Torture Chamber
John Swain
Noel Douglas, 1931

Luxurious Bathing
Andrew White Tuer
Field & Tuer, 1879

The Book of Practical Candle Magic
Leo Vinci
Wellingborough: Aquarian Press, 1981

Careers in Dope
Dan Waldorf
Englewood Cliffs, NJ: Prentice-Hall, 1973

The Famines of the World
Cornelius Walford
Edward Stanford, 1879
An exhaustive listing, starting in 1708 BC.

Naseology; or, Notes on Noses
Eden Warwick*
A. Bentley, 1852
(*The pseudonym of George Jabet.)

Ice Carving Professionally
George Philip Weising
Fairfield, Conn.: n.p., 1954

A Practical Guide for Inspectors of Nuisances
F. R. Wilson
Knight & Co., 1891 (2nd edition)

Rock Stars in Their Underpants
Paula Yates
Virgin Books, 1980

Julius Caesar and His Public Image
Zvi Yavetz
Ithaca, NY: Cornell University Press, 1982; Thames & Hudson, 1983

The Influence of Mountains Upon the Development of Human Intelligence
Geoffrey Winthrop Young
Glasgow: Jackson, Son & Co. and Glasgow University Press, 1957

Lappish Bear Graves in Northern Sweden
Inge Zachrisson and Elizabeth Iregren
Stockholm: Almqvist & Wiksell, 1974

Earth-shaking Songs
Professor Xu Yuan Zhong (trans.)
Hong Kong: The Commercial Press Ltd, 1981

Merit Award for Books on Extraordinarily Specialized Subjects

This coveted award goes to **Berthold Laufer** of Chicago (1874–1934), the distinguished author of a veritable library of over 100 fascinating works, mostly published in Leiden by E. J. Brill or Chicago by the Field Museum of Natural History, including (in chronological order of publication):

1899
Petroglyphs on the Amoor

1906
The Bird Chariot

1912

Confucius and His Portraits
The Discovery of a Lost Book
History of the Finger-print System

1913

The Application of the Tibetan Sexagenary Cycle
Arabic and Chinese Trade in Walrus & Narwhal Ivory

1914

Was Oderic of Pordenone Ever in Tibet?
The Sexagenary Cycle Once More
Three Tokhavian Bagatelles
Bird Divination Among the Tibetans

1915

The Eskimo Screw as a Culture–Historical Problem
Asbestos and Salamander

1916

Cardan's Suspension in China

1917

The Reindeer and Its Domestication
Loan-Words in Tibetan

1923

Use of Human Skulls and Bones in Tibet
Oriental Theatricals

1925

Chinese Baskets

1926

**Ostrich Egg-shell Cups of Mesopotamia and the Ostrich in
Ancient and Modern Times**

1927

Insect Musicians and Cricket Champions of China
Agate *(section on archaeology and folklore by Laufer)*

1928
The Giraffe in History and Art

1930
Felt: How It Was Made and Used in Ancient Times
Geophagy [earth-eating]

1931
The Domestication of the Cormorant in China and Japan

1938 *(Posthumous)*
American Plant Migration

Whisker's World

For the benefit of readers who may wish to pursue this rewarding field via the works of its leading writers, we have pleasure in offering this selective bibliography of pogonology.

Beard Shaving, and the Common Use of the Razor, an Unnatural, Irrational, Unmanly, Ungodly and Fatal Fashion Among Christians
Anon. (identified as William Henry Henslowe)
W. E. Painter, 1847

Pro Sacerdotum Barbis
Giovanni Pierio Valeriano Bolzani
Rome: n.p., 1531
Argues the case for priests wearing beards.

Rhythmical Essays on the Beard Question
W. Carter
n.p., 1868

Pogonologia; or, A Philosophical and Historical Essay on Beards
Jacques Antoine Dulaure
Exeter: Printed by R. Thorn; sold by T. Cadell, 1786
"A man without a beard would be much less surprising now-a-days, than a bearded woman, which proves how unnatural our tastes and customs are."

How to Shave Yourself
"An Expert"
Van & Alexander, 1906

49

The Philosophy of Beards
Thomas S. Gowing
Ipswich: J. Haddock, c. 1850

Concerning Beards
Edwin Valentine Mitchell
New York: Dodd, Mead & Co., 1930

The Mysteries, Secrets and Whole Art of an Easy Shave
Joseph Morton
L. U. Grill, 1893

Ancient and Modern Beards
G. Price
n.p., 1893

Some Account of the Beard and the Moustachio
John Adey Repton
J. B. Nichols, 1839

Beards
Reginald Reynolds
Allen & Unwin, 1950

Barbalogia
Guiseppe Valeriano de Vannetti
Roveredo: n.p., 1759
Goes into the problem of whether Adam was born with a beard, coming down in favour of those who hold that "The father of the human race had a beard from the first instant of his life. All men, before the Flood, had one too."

The Folly and Evil of Shaving
"Xerxes"
n.p., 1854

Facts at Your Fingertips
There are certain reference books that no home should be without, among them:

Bibliography of Mangrove Research, 1600–1975
Anon.
Paris: UNESCO, 1981

The Great Encyclopedia of Universal Knowledge*
Anon.
Odhams, 1933
(*A small octavo book.)

How To Do It; or, Directions for Knowing or Doing Everything Needful
Anon.
New York: J. F. Tingley, 1864

An Illustrated Inventory of Famous Dismembered Works of Art
Anon.
Paris: UNESCO, 1974

Liver Building, Liverpool. List of Stop Cocks
Anon.
Toxteth: J. Litchfield (Printer), 1912

Celebrated in song and television soap opera, the Liver Birds spread their wings above Liverpool docks, symbolizing Merseyside for millions. But what of the stop cocks essential to the smooth running of the Liver Building that supports them?

Here is the long-lost record – perhaps the only surviving testimonial to their place in history – with the ownership inscription of "W. Griffiths & Sons, Plumbers, &c.", who undoubtedly held the responsible position of stop-cock turners in the case of emergency. Only here can be discovered the fact that stop cock No. 2 on the tenth floor, bottom tank, south side, shuts off the gentlemen's lavatories and bar, and that the cisterns in the National Health Section Offices on the ground floor can be found on iron girders behind the lifts one floor up.

LIVER BUILDING,

LIVERPOOL.

List of Stop Cocks.

The unique plumbers' reference copy, listing over 130 stop cocks with their precise locations.

RUBBING ALONG
IN BURMESE

Published By the
DIRECTORATE OF WELFARE
AND EDUCATION
Adjutant General's Branch, G. H. Q., Simla

NOT TO BE PUBLISHED

The information given in this publication is not to be communicated
either directly or indirectly, to the Press or to any person not
holding an official position in His Majesty's Service.

PRINTED BY THE MANAGER, GOVERNMENT OF INDIA PRESS, SIMLA
1944

"Not to be Published" and "not to be communicated" either, making for hopelessly one-sided conversations, guaranteed to rub up all Burmese the wrong way.

Rubbing Along in Burmese

Anon.

Simla: Directorate of Welfare and Education, Adjutant General's Branch GHQ, 1944

Who's Who in Cocker Spaniels

Marion Frances Robinson Mangrum (compiler)

Norman?, Okla.: n.p., 1944

Early Victorian Water Engineers

Geoffrey Morse Binnie

Thomas Telford, 1981

The New Guide of the Conversation in Portuguese and English in Two Parts

Pedro Carolino

Peking "And to the house of All the booksellers of Paris", 1869 (2nd edition)

This phrase book reaches a level of brilliance quite unsurpassed by any other. Portuguese–English conversations are intelligently constructed by the author, whose tools are French–English and French–Portuguese dictionaries. The result squares the triangle of languages uniquely and effectively:

‘A choice of *familiar dialogues*, clean of gallicisms, and despoiled phrases, it was missing yet to studious portuguese and brazillian Youth; and also to persons of other nations, that wish to know the portuguese language. We sought all we may do, to correct that want, composing and divising the present little work in two parts. The first includes a greatest vocabulary proper names by alphabetical order; and the second forty three *Dialogues* adapted to the usual precisions of life. For that reason we did put, with a scrupulous exactness, a great variety own expressions to english and portuguese idioms; without to attach us selves (as make some others) almost at a literal translation; translation what only will be for to accustom the portuguese pupils, or-foreign, to speak very bad any of the mentioned idioms.

We were increasing this second edition with a phraseology, in the first part, and some familiar letters, anecdotes, idiotisms, proverbs, and to second a coin's index.

The *Works* which we were confering for this labour, fond use us for nothing; but those what were publishing to Portugal, or out, they were almost all composed for some foreign, or some national little aquainted in the spirit of both languages. It was resulting from that corelessness to rest these *Works* fill of imperfections, and anomolies of style; in spite of the infinite typographical faults which some times, invert the sense of the periods. It increase not to contain any of those *Works* the figured pronunciation of the english words, nor the prosodical accent in the portuguese: indispensable object whom wish to speak the english and portuguese languages correctly.

We expect then, who the little book (for the care what we wrote him, and her typographical correction) that may be worth the acceptation of the studios persons, and especially of the Youth, at which we dedicate him particularly.’ (From the preface. *Sic* throughout!)

THE NEW GUIDE

OF THE

CONVERSATION

IN PORTUGUESE AND ENGLISH

IN TWO PARTS

BY

PEDRO CAROLINO

The title-page of Carolino's classic phrase book gives just a hint of things to come.

Jews at a Glance
Mac Davis
New York: Hebrew Publishing Co., 1956
From Abraham to Adolph Zukor, "pioneer with a magic lantern".

The Irish Word Processing Guide
Dolores Donovan and Diarmuid Herlihy (eds.)
Dublin: Hamilton Press, 1981

Six Language Dictionary of Plastics and Rubber Technology
A. F. Dorian
Iliffe, 1965

The Encyclopedia of Medical Ignorance
Ronald Duncan and M. Weston-Smith (eds.)
Oxford: Pergamon Press, 1984

Encyclopedia of Pocket Knives
Roy Ehrhardt
Kansas City: Heart of America Press, n.d. (3 vols.)

Biographical Dictionary of Irishmen in France
Richard Francis Hayes
Dublin: M. H. Gill & Son, 1949
Mr Hayes was also author of the more specialist

Irish Swordsmen of France
Dublin: M. H. Gill & Son, 1934

Sea Terms and Phrases: English–Spanish: Spanish–English
Graham Hewlett
Charles Griffin, 1907

Abbott's Encyclopedia of Rope Tricks
Stewart James
Colon, Mich.: Abbott's Magic Novelty Co., 1945

Messing Records, 1272–1803
Oswald Greenwaye Knapp
Society of Genealogists, 1937

and also:

The Parish Registers of Piddlehinton, Co. Dorset, 1539–1653
Society of Geneaologists, 1938

A Catalogue of Swedish Local Postage Stamps, Issued from 1941 to 1947
Raymond George Lister
Dumfries: K. Jahr, 1952

Five Hundred Questions on Subjects Requiring Investigation in the Social Condition of Natives of India
Revd J. Long
Calcutta: Baptist Mission Press, 1862
Questions answered include: "Are dwarfs numerous?", "Spitting, why practiced so much by Hindus?", "What are the recreations of females – is kite-flying such?" and "In what respects are boatmen equal to sailors?"

Prominent People of New Brunswick
Charles Herbert MacLean
Saint John, NB: The Biographical Society of Canada, 1937

Railway Literature, 1556–1830
Robert Alexander Peddie
Grafton & Co., 1931
Covers the interesting period in railway history before trains were invented.

The Encyclopedia of Alcoholism
Robert O'Brien and Morris Chafetz
Bicester: Facts on File, 1983

How to Abandon Ship
Philip Richards and John J. Banigan
New York: Cornell Maritime Press, 1942 (2nd edition)

Essential – but somewhat alarming – reading for those on Atlantic convoy duty during World War II.

Biographical Dictionary of Wax Modellers
Edward Pyke
Oxford: Oxford University Press (Vol. 1), 1973; The Author (Vols. 2 and 3), 1983

Prostitutes of Hyderabad
M. Rangarao
Hyderabad: Hyderabad Association for Moral and Social Hygiene, 1970

A Dictionary of International Slurs
A. A. Roback
Cambridge, Mass.: Sci-Art Publishers, 1944

Manuale di Conversazione: Italiano–Groenlandese
Ciro Sozio and Mario Fantin
Bologna: Tamari Editori, 1962

The Proverbs of British Guiana
Revd James Speirs
Demerara: The Argosy Co., 1902
'No. 539: Luck mo' bettah dan han'some.
No. 772: Rum Done, Fun Done.'

Selective Bibliography of the Literature of Lubrication
Nathan Van Patten and Grace S. Lewis
Kingston, Ont.: N. Van Patten, 1926

1001 Things You Can Get Free
Mort Weisinger
New York: Bantam, 1957
"A Fabulous New Treasury of America's Choicest Giveaway Items", including:

'Ever envy the way the heroes in Hollywood films achieve that well-groomed look by the perfect way they knot their tie? It's easy to obtain the same effect, if you know how. For an illustrated brochure on how to tie a better knot, send for "Tie Lore Booklet" . . . .

Free Psychoanalysis for Pets in Los Angeles. 250,000 dogs are in need of a psychoanalyst estimates the L.A. Society for the Prevention of Cruelty to Animals . . . .

Free movie to show in your own home: "Lifeline". Action picture which stars famous actor Thomas Mitchell and tells the exciting story of rope and twine.'

7
Marvels of Science
Boffins' brilliant books

Petroleum in Leather
Anon.
Rochester, NY: Vacuum Oil Co., 1896

The Coming Disaster Worse Than the H-bomb,
Astronomically, Geologically and Scientifically Proven. The Coal Beds, Ice Ages, Tides, and Coming Soon, a Great Wave and Flood Caused by a Shift of the Axis of the Earth From the Gyroscopic Action of Our Solar System. Why Our Solar System Works.
Adam D. Barber
Washington, DC: Barber Scientific Foundation, 1954
Barber's theory is that the Earth shifts on its axis every 9000 years, taking a mere ninety minutes to do so. The last occasion resulted in Noah's Flood; the next is imminent . . . .

The Biochemist's Songbook
Harold Baum
Oxford: Pergamon Press, 1982
This successful, albeit improbable, combination has been followed by Baum's *Biorhythms* (*Learn Through Music*, 1984) in which O-level biology is set to words and music. Part 1: Human Biology; Part 2: General Biology:

‛At last the ultimate best seller, sing-along-a-syllabus. These two sensational new packages take biology into a dimension never thought possible. Subjects such as excretion, reproduction, genetics, and evolution have been set to words by the world's leading [only?] exponent of the biological ballad, Professor Harold Baum and original music written by Peter Shade. Each package contains a book plus an audio cassette with the songs sung by a new group, *The Metabolites*.’

Arresting Disclosures. A Report on the Strange Findings in Undergarments Washed with Soap and Water, and Popularly Supposed to be Clean, Fresh and Wholesome
John A. Bolton
Leicester: J. & J. H. Vice, 1924
A copy of this book has been seen in a bookseller's catalogue described as good, "but not spotless".

Water, Not Convex: the Earth Not a Globe!
William Carpenter
The Author, 1871
and again:

One Hundred Proofs that the Earth is Not a Globe
Baltimore: The Author, 1885
Carpenter was a British follower of "Parallax" (see page 59) and later emigrated to America to promote his Flat Earth Theory.

Atomic Bombing: How to Protect Yourself
Davis Watson, etc.
New York: Wise & Co., Inc., 1950
"A Wise Publication".

❛"Radioactivity is like a dog shaking itself after being in the water."

"Steaks are a must in the diet of the burn patient."

"American skyscrapers . . . are built on heavy steel frames. Buildings such as these . . . would withstand the blast of an atomic bomb."

"Curl up in a ball as you hit the ground."❜

Romping Through Physics
Otto Willi Gail
G. Routledge & Sons, 1933

What's Wanted. A List of 895 Needed Inventions
Institute of Patentees
Institute of Patentees, c. 1933 (3rd edition)
A useful source of ideas for the budding inventor: lipstick-proof linen; a bullet-proof stroboscope; an automatic refrigerator for under £3.10s.0d.; a machine for the dining table to pick winkles from their shells; improvements in deckchairs which allow the user to sit sideways; a slot-machine for use at post offices to give two halfpennies for a penny; and, perhaps most useful of all, a domestic machine for use in private houses for getting rid of books by pulping.

How to Draw a Straight Line
Sir Alfred Bray Kempe
Macmillan, 1877
"The Unexplored Fields are still vast."

The Human Gyroscope:
A Consideration of the Gyroscopic Rotation of the Earth as Mechanism of the Evolution of Terrestrial Living Forms. Explaining the Phenomenon of Sex: Its Origin and Development and Its Significance in the Evolutionary Process
Arabella Kenealy
Hudson & Keans, 1934

Flights of Fancy: Early Aviation in Battersea and Wandsworth
Patrick Loobey
Recreation Department, Wandsworth Borough Council, 1981
Revealing the astonishing information that the Wright Brothers were busy building
aeroplanes in Battersea, south London, in the early 1900s. However, these were not
the Wright Brothers, Wilbur and Orville, but two *other* Wright Brothers, Howard
and Warwick. Not many people know that . . . .

Fuzzy Reasoning and Its Applications
E. H. Mamdani and B. R. Gaines (eds.)
Academic Press, 1981

Light and Truth,
M's Invention for Destroying All Foul Air and Fire Damp in Coal Pits (Proving Also) the Scriptures to be Right which Learned Men are Mystifying, and Proving the Orang Outang or Monkey the Most Unlikely Thing Under the Sun to be the Serpent That Beguiled Our First Parents
Jonathan Martin
n.p., n.d.
Jonathan Martin (1782–1838), the brother of John Martin, the painter of apoca-
lyptic scenes, arranged a mini-apocalypse of his own in 1829 by setting fire to York
Minster.

Zetetic Astronomy
"Parallax"*
Birmingham: W. Cornish, 1849
(*The pseudonym of Samuel Birley Rowbotham.)
In a series of experiments conducted along the "Bedford Level" in Cambridgeshire
in 1838, "Parallax" attempted to demonstrate that he could see distant objects
sited on the canal and that cannon balls fired vertically fell straight down, thus
proving that the Earth is flat and non-rotating. His findings were published in this
erudite work, the title of which derives from the Greek, meaning "I discover for
myself". He had many zetetic followers, including William Carpenter (see page 58),
Lady Elizabeth Anne Mould Blount, John Hampden, William Edgell and others
who wrote books along similar lines, starting a "Flat Earth" cult that continues to
this day.

The Romance of the Holes in Bread: a Plea for the Recognition of the Scientific Laboratory as the Testing Place for Truth
I. K. Russell
Easton, Pa.: The Chemical Publishing Co., 1924

A New General Theory of the Teeth of Wheels
Edward Sang
A. & C. Black, 1852
Sang was professor of Mechanical Philosophy in the Imperial School, Muhendis-
Hana Berrii, Constantinople.

Chemistrianity. (Popular Knowledge of Chemistry) A Poem;
Also an Oratorical Verse on each known Chemical Element in the Universe, Giving Descriptions, Properties, Sources, Preparation and Chief Uses
John Carrington Sellars
Birkenhead: The Author, c. 1873

Seven Years of 'Manifold': 1968–1980
Ian Stewart and John Jaworski (eds.)
Nantwich: Shiva Publishing, c. 1981

Articles on mathematical problems – including, perhaps, how 1980 minus 1968 equals seven?

The Diseases of Electrical Machinery
George Wilfred Stubbings
E. & F. N. Spon, 1939

Cleaning Up Coal
Gerhard Webber
New York: Harper & Row, 1982

If you think coal is nasty, dirty stuff, this is the book for you.

A Study of Splashes
Arthur Mason Worthington
Longmans, Green, 1908

Notable for the depth of its investigations into a subject that is inherently of no interest to anyone, *A Study of Splashes* describes with near-obsessive attention to detail the astonishing spectacle of a "water drop weighing 0.4 grams falling 137 cm (4½ feet) into milk mixed with water". Optimistically aiming it at "the general reader", Arthur Worthington explains how his *magnum opus* grew out of his 1894 Royal Institution lecture, "The Splash of a Drop", which was reprinted in the *Romance of Science* series, published – perhaps surprisingly – by the Society for the Promotion of Christian Knowledge. As headmaster and professor of Physics at the Royal Naval Engineering College, Devonport, he might be expected to have taken an interest in the effect of projectiles falling into water – but as most of the objects described are ball-bearings falling into milk, the relevance to naval engineering is not immediately apparent. His suggested experiments would also probably result in raised eyebrows at the average tea party:

> ‘Let the reader when he next receives a cup of tea or coffee to which no milk has yet been added, make the simple experiment of dropping into it from a spoon, at the height of fifteen or sixteen inches above the surface, a single drop of milk.’

This extraordinary book contains no fewer than 197 photographs, all of which are virtually identical – as is the cover picture, embossed in gold on elegant green cloth – and appear to show drops of milk falling into cups of tea. "More tea, Vicar – and I wonder if you'd be interested in a little experiment. . . ?"

8
England's True Wealth
Books on manure – and worse

An Essay Upon Wind; with Curious Anecdotes of Eminent Peteurs. Humbly Dedicated to the Lord Chancellor
Anon. (alleged to be Charles James Fox)
"Printed and sold by all the Booksellers in Town and Country", *1787*

In case there might be any misunderstanding of the title, and the subject matter of this delightful little pamphlet be taken to be of some meteorological significance, the author soon makes it clear that this is, undeniably, "An Essay on Farting".

> ❝I take it there are five or six different species of Farts, and which are perfectly distinct from each other, both in weight, and smell.
> > First, the sonorous, and full-toned Fart;
> > Second, the double Fart;
> > Third, the soft-fizzing Fart;
> > Fourth, the wet Fart;
> > and Fifth, the sullen, wind bound Fart.❞

The noble author proceeds to propose "the following efforts to produce them, and I have little doubt that they will be happily, and satisfactorily procured". Viz:

> ❝Fart No. 4 – Commonly called the wet Fart, is very easily procured. Let any person fond of overeating, cram himself with pies, custards, whip-sylabub, prunes, &c. &c. and he will do his business with effectual dispatch, so as to need an immediate washing. Ladies produce this species of Fart better than gentlemen, so that it is adviseable to try this experiment upon a strong, healthy young lady of about eighteen, and who is apt to be hungry.❞

The "Afterthoughts upon Farting shewing its great utility; with curious Anecdotes of Eminent Farters" gives warning of overindulgence in the art by quoting the case of Simon Tup, "the Farting Blacksmith" from Kirkeaton, Yorkshire, who

> ❝had the singular and ingenious talent of accompanying any instrument . . . which he could perform so admirably in time, tone and tune, as to deceive the nicest judges. . . . The fate of this poor fellow was very melancholy; by an uncommon exertion which he made in the famous song "Blow high, blow low", he unfortunately broke a blood-vessel of which he instantly died.❞

But despite the possible dangers of excess *a posteriori*,

> ❝the utility and comfort of Farting, then, all the world must allow. . . . Fart away then, my brethren, and let Farting be in common among you . . . FART LOUD I SAY, and never more be restrained. . . .❞

61

With volumes like these, there is not even the necessity to follow Lord Chesterfield's advice to his son to read books before using their pages for another, more basic, function.

Stray Leaves from Japanese Papers
Anon.
Bourne, Johnson & Latimer, c. 1870

The ultimate lavatory book. Approximately 400 blank leaves of

'Japanese sanitary paper. Antiseptic. Hygienic. A Perfectly pure article for the toilet and lavatory, and a preventative for piles . . . as soft as silk and although it is very tough, will readily dissolve in water . . . confidently recommended as the best article ever produced for the particular purpose for which it is intended.'

Also, from the same publishers, but in paper covers rather than maroon cloth, *Nothing but Leaves* (n.d.).

Sewers
Edward Vaughan Bevan and Bernard Trevelyan Rees
Chapman & Hall, 1937

The Urine Dance of the Zuni Indians of New Mexico

Captain John G. Bourke

Ann Arbor, Mich.: American Association for the Advancement of Science, 1885

In this brief account John Bourke, a captain in the US Army Third Cavalry, describes how on 17 November 1881 he was taken as a guest to witness a singular ritual known as the "urine dance". Twelve Zuni Indian dancers, some wearing cotton nightcaps and one, appropriately, in an india-rubber coat, entered and sang an obscene ditty: "their song was apparently a ludicrous reference to everything and everybody in sight". Having thus taken the piss out of their audience, they proceeded to make it: an "olla" (a kind of cooking pot) containing urine was brought in ceremoniously, "of which the filthy brutes drank heartily". This appetizer was followed by a tin pail containing over two gallons of urine, which the performers guzzled with apparent relish.

Captain Bourke was assured that on other occasions the rite was extended to the consumption of excrement, but this was too much for him and, without waiting to test the truth of the claim, he made an excuse and left.

The urine dance clearly made a lasting impression on Captain Bourke, for in 1891 he published a detailed treatise, *Scatalogical Rites of all Nations* (Washington, DC: W. H. Lowdermilk). This learned tome is subtitled, "A Dissertation upon the Employment of Excrementitious Remedial Agents in Religion, Therapeutics, Divination, Witchcraft, Love-Philters, &c." The title-page bears the legend, "NOT FOR GENERAL PERUSAL".

Scatalogical Rites contains a wealth of fascinating detail, including a description of a novel method of curing tobacco:

> ‘The best varieties of tobacco coming from America were arranged in bunches, tied to stakes, and suspended in privies, in order that the fumes arising from the human ordure and urine might correct the corrupt and noxious principles in the plant in the crude state.’

Danger. Government Health Warning. Cigarettes Can Seriously Damage Your Health. And little wonder.

A Sanitary Crusade Through the East and Australia

Robert Boyle

Glasgow: Boyle, 1892

The Muck Manual: a Practical Treatise on the Nature and Value of Manures

F. Falkner

John Murray, 1843

Arse Musica; or, The Lady's Back Report to Don Fart-in-Hand-o Puff-in Dorst . . . on the Benefit of Farting

Countess of Frizzle Rumpff

"Printed for A. Moore, near St. Paul's", 1722

The Sewage Question
Frederick Charles Krepp
Longmans, Green, 1867
What's the answer?

The Law Relating to Sewers and Drains
Alexander Macmorran and W. Addington Willis
Butterworth, 1904

How to Test Your Urine at Home
B. C. Meyrowitz
Girard, Ka.: Haldeman-Julius, c. 1935

The Benefit of Farting Explain'd
Fart-inhando Puff-indorst*
"Printed for A. Moore, near St. Paul's", 1727
(*Pseudonym – probably Jonathan Swift.)

The BENEFIT of

FARTING

EXPLAIN'D:

OR, THE

FUNDAMENT-all *CAUSE* of the
Diſtempers incident to the Fair Sex.

Inquir'd into :

Proving *à Poſteriori* moſt of the *Diſordures*
in-*tail'd* on, them are owing to *Flatulencies* not ſeaſon-
ably vented.

Wrote in *Spaniſh*, by Don *Fart-inhando Puff-
indorſt* Profeſſor of *Bumbaſt* in the Univerſity of *Craccow*.

AND

Tranſlated into *Engliſh* at the Requeſt and for the Uſe of the
Lady *Damp-Fart*, of *Her-fart-ſhire*.

A FART, tho' wholeſome does not fail,	*Thus Gun-powder confin'd, you know Sir,*
If barr'd of Paſſage by the Tail,	*Crows ſtronger, as 'tis ram'd the cloſer;*
To fly back to the Head again,	*But, if in open Air it fires,*
And by its Fumes diſturb the Brain :	*In harmleſs Smoke its Force expires.*

The THIRTEENTH EDITION, *with Additions, revis'd by a College*
of Phyzz-icians, *and approved by ſeveral Ladies of* Quality.

LONDON :
Printed for *A. Moore*, near St. *Paul's*, and Sold by the Book-
ſellers, 1727.

A dozen Swiftian puns are crammed into the finest title-page of the eighteenth century.

Mrs Sheil's throwaway twopenny pamphlet, described by one reviewer as "garbage".

End Product
Daniel Sabbath and Mandel Hall
New York: Urizen Books, 1977

Dust and the Dustbin
Mrs Sheil
Home and Colonial School Society, n.d.
Mrs Sheil is described as "Lecturer, for the Ladies' Sanitary Association and the National Health Society".

Goodbye to the Flush Toilet
Carol Hupping Stoner
Emmaus, Pa.: Rodale, 1984

DANGERS TO HEALTH:

A PICTORIAL GUIDE

TO

DOMESTIC

SANITARY DEFECTS,

BY

T. PRIDGIN TEALE, M.A.,

SURGEON TO THE GENERAL INFIRMARY AT LEEDS.

FOURTH EDITION.

LONDON:
J. & A. CHURCHILL, NEW BURLINGTON STREET,
CHARLES GOODALL, COOKRIDGE STREET, AND BOAR LANE, LEEDS.
1883.

PLATE XXXII.

How people drink sewage.—No. I.
Drain leaking into a well.

F

Dangers to Health: a Pictorial Guide to Domestic Sanitary Defects

T. Pridgin Teale

J. & A. Churchill, 1878

In chapters with graphic titles such as "How People Drink Sewage", Mr Teale describes in appalling detail the way in which undesirable ingredients are accidentally added to drinking water.

Constipation and Our Civilization

James Charles Thomson

Thorsons Publishers, 1943

'The connection between our Indigestion and our indecision; Our Food and our Behaviour. Advertising Specialists, Pain, Drugs and Enemas. . . .

I was discussing soured tissues with Henry Lynch, a Canadian engineer, at that time owner of the Marvel Cave in the Ozarks, Missouri, and also something of a biologist in his spare time. . . .'

On the Composition of Farmyard Manure

Dr Augustus Voelcker
Printed by W. Clowes & Sons, 1856.
And another to dip into:

On Liquid Manure

Printed by W. Clowes & Sons, 1859

England's True Wealth

William White
Groombridge & Sons, 1849

This is one of the most extraordinary justifications of the saying, "You can't tell a book by looking at the cover." The original binding is sumptuous green watered silk, lettered in gilt, *England's True Wealth*. It gives the clear impression of being a scarce pamphlet on banking or economics, probably by a wealthy politician rich enough to garb his random thoughts in an almost regal cloak.

In fact, the full title on the title-page reads: *England's True Wealth; or, Foecal [faecal] Matters in Their Application to Agriculture by William White, Consulting Chemist to the City of London Portable Manure Company.*

ENGLAND'S TRUE WEALTH;

OR,

FŒCAL MATTERS

IN THEIR

APPLICATION TO AGRICULTURE.

BY

WILLIAM WHITE,

LECTURER ON AGRICULTURAL CHEMISTRY,
MEMBER OF THE ROYAL AGRICULTURAL SOCIETY,
CONSULTING CHEMIST TO THE CITY OF LONDON PORTABLE MANURE COMPANY,
AND LATE HON. SEC. TO THE YORK FARMERS' CLUB.

The Wonderful World of Nature

Weird books on plants and animals

An Essay Towards the Character of the Late Chimpanzee, Who Died Feb. 23, 1738–9
Anon.
n.p., 1739

Harnessing the Earthworm
Thomas J. Barrett
Faber & Faber, 1949

Blood Histamine Levels in Swine Following Total Body X-Radiation and a Flash Burn
Hamilton A. Baxter
Reprinted from Annals of Surgery, *1954*

HARNESSING THE EARTHWORM

A practical inquiry into soil-building, soil conditioning, and plant nutrition through the action of earthworms, with instructions for intensive propagation and use of Domesticated Earthworms in biological soil-building

by

THOMAS J. BARRETT

with an introduction by
E. B. BALFOUR

Thomas J. Barrett's guide to the breaking of wild, untamed worms.

Development of the Female Genital Tract in the American Opossum
James S. Baxter
Washington, DC: Carnegie Institution of Washington, 1935

Dung Fungi: an Illustrated Guide to Coprophilous Fungi in New Zealand
Ann Bell
Wellington: Victoria University Press, 1984

The Psychic Life of Micro-Organisms
Alfred Binet
Longman & Co., 1889

Adventures with Small Animals
Owen Bishop
Murray, 1982

Black-Footed Ferret Recovery Plan
Black-Footed Ferret Recovery Team
Washington, DC: US Fish & Wildlife Service, 1978

Animals as Criminals
J. Brand
Reprinted from Pearson's Magazine, *1896*

The Story of a California Rabbit Drive
S. Ervin Chapman
New York: Fleming H. Ravell, 1910
Comparison with a beetle drive is erroneous. Rabbits are herded into pens and then clubbed to death.

Psychology of Botany
"Charubel"
Tyldesley: R. Welch, 1906

Carnivorous Butterflies
Austin Hobart Clark
Washington, DC: United States Government Printing Office, 1926

Swine Judging for Beginners
Joel Simmonds Coffey
Columbus, Ohio: Ohio State University, 1915

Do Snakes Have Legs?
Bert Cunningham
New York: Reprinted from Scientific Monthly, *1934*

Frog Raising for Pleasure and Profit
Dr Albert Broel*
New Orleans, La.: Marlboro House, 1950
(*Described as the "Originator of Canned Frog Legs".)
With an extensive collection of recipes, including "Dominant Mayonnaise Dressing for Giant Frogs"; "Jellied Giant Bullfrog Creamed Salad"; and "Minced Giant Bullfrog Savoury Sandwiches".

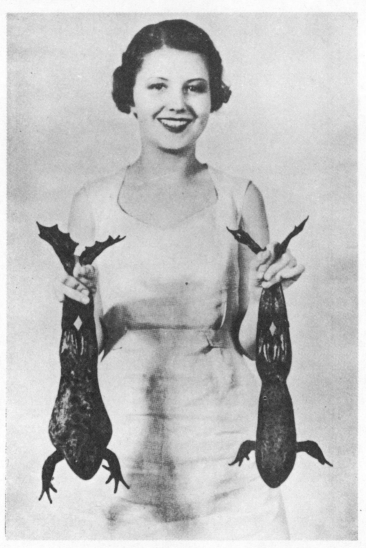

A Comparison Between the Young Lady and the Bullfrogs.
She is holding Female in one hand and the Male in the other.

Beauty and the Beasts: this pleasurable pin-up from Broel's Frog Raising for Pleasure and Profit *gives no clue to the profitable fate that awaits the Young Lady's friends.*

The Common Teasel as a Carnivorous Plant
Miller Christy
Journal of Botany, *1922*

THE COMMON TEASEL AS A CARNIVOROUS PLANT

By MILLER CHRISTY, F.L.S.

LONDON :
Reprinted from the "JOURNAL OF BOTANY," vol. lxi.
1922.

The terrifying story of the man-eating teasel. All right: insects, very small ones – possibly.

Comprehensive Utilization of the Milk-thistle
The Editing Group of the "Comprehensive Utilization of the Milk-thistle"
Beijing: Science Press, 1982

New Guinea Tapeworms and Jewish Grandmothers
Robert S. Desowitz
New York: Norton, 1981

Ants and Some Other Insects: an Enquiry into the Psychic Power of These Animals
Auguste Henri Forel (trans. William Morton Wheeler)
Chicago, Ill.: The Open Court Publishing Co., 1904

Darwin's Negro Bird-stuffer
R. B. Freeman
Royal Society, 1978

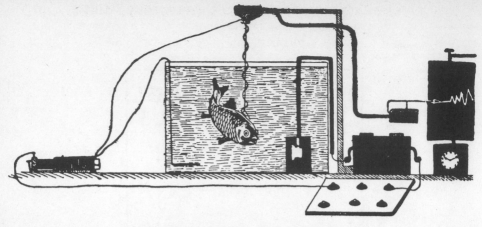

A Fish answers the telephone

A technological breakthrough that was never fully exploited: in this prototype answering machine a fish is trained to say "He's on the other line."

Fish Who Answer the Telephone
Yury Petrovich Frolov
Kegan Paul, Trench, Trubner, 1937

The Color of Horses
Ben K. Green
Flagstaff, Ariz.: Northland Press, 1983

The Ants of Colorado
Robert Edmond Gregg
Boulder, Colo.: University of Colorado Press, 1963

Ferret Facts and Fancies
A. R. Harding
Columbus, Ohio: The Author, 1915

The Goldfish of China in the 18th Century
George John Frangopulo Hervey
China Society, 1950

The Sleep of Plants
John Hill
Printed for R. Baldwin, 1757

Anaesthesia & Narcosis of Animals and Birds
Sir Frederick Thomas George Hobday
Baillière & Co., 1915
and:

Castration
Edinburgh: W. & A. K. Johnston, 1914 (2nd edition)

Did a Hen or an Egg Exist First? or, My Talks with a Sceptic
Jacob Horner
Religious Tract Society, 1892

Gigantic Cuttle-fish
William Saville Kent
Boston, Mass.: Estes & Lauriat, 1879

The Direction of Hair in Animals and Man
Walter Kidd
Adam & Charles Black, 1903

Digestion in the Pig
D. E. Kidder and M. J. Manners
Bath: John Wright, 1978

Studies on Bunt or Stinking Smut
Robert Whilmer Leukel
Washington, DC: United States Department of Agriculture, 1937
A report on ways to reduce the incidence of these diseases of wheat crops. However,

‘while many of the fifty tested bunt fungicides controlled bunt in the experiments, most of them must be eliminated because of excessive cost, extreme poisonousness, corrosiveness, hydroscopicity, injury to seed, rapid deterioration or unavailability. . . .’

Crab, Shrimp and Lobster Lore
William Barry Lord
George Routledge & Sons, 1867

The Onion Maggot
Arthur L. Lovett
Corvallis, Oreg.: Agricultural Experimental Station, 1923

A Veterinary Materia Medica and Clinical Repertory with a Materia Medica of the Nosodes
George Macleod
C. W. Daniel & Co., 1983

Favourite Flies and Their Histories
Mary Orvis Marbury
Boston, Mass.: Charles T. Branford & Co., 1955

Full Revelations of a Professional Rat-catcher after 25 Years’ Experience
Ike Matthews
Manchester: Friendly Societies’ Printing Co., 1898

The Home-Life and Economic Status of the Double-Crested Cormorant
Howard Lewis Mendall
Orono, Me.: University Press, 1936

Handbook of Common New Guinea Frogs
J. I. Menzies
Wau: Wau Ecology Institute Handbook No. 1, 1976

Memorandum on the Size, Sex and Condition of Lobsters
Ministry of Agriculture and Fisheries
HMSO, 1912
This report is described as being "For Official Use" only. Full of interesting tables such as: "Table (xii) – Number of Non-berried Lobsters Carrying Threads on Swimming Legs. Sussex, 1908–09."

Characteristics of the Conditioned Response in Cretinous Rats
Garrett W. Morrison and Bert Cunningham
Baltimore, Md.: Reprinted from The Journal of Comparative Psychology, *1941*

The Joy of Chickens
Dennis Nolan
Englewood Cliffs, NJ: Prentice-Hall, 1981
"A history and celebration of the chicken, rare and common."
(Publisher's catalogue.)

Sexual Interactions in Eukaryotic Microbes
Danton H. O'Day and Paul A. Horgen (eds.)
Academic Press, 1981

Life and Love in the Aquarium
C. H. Peters
New York: The Empire Tropical Fish Import Co., 1934

Stress and Fish
A. D. Pickering (ed.)
Academic Press, 1981

Proceedings of the Second International Workshop on Nude Mice
Tokyo: University of Tokyo Press, 1978

Carrots Love Tomatoes
Louise Riotte
Charlotte, Vt.: Garden Way, 1981

Enjoy Your Chameleon
Earl Schneider
New York: The Pet Library, n.d.

The Art of Faking Exhibition Poultry
George Riley Scott
T. Werner Laurie, 1934
The author treads an indistinct line between condemning this widespread and despicable practice, and telling the reader exactly how to do it. It includes one crucial piece of advice: "Always wear rubber gloves". Mr Scott also tells us:

The Truth About Poultry
Poultry Press, 1927

THE ART OF FAKING EXHIBITION POULTRY

GEORGE R. SCOTT

T. WERNER LAURIE LTD.
Cobham House, 24 & 26, Water Lane, London, E.C. 4

Elements of the Organic Enamel of the Hedgehog
John Silness
Bergen: Universitetsforlaget, 1967

The Genitalia of Bombyliidae
O. Theodor
Jerusalem: Israel Academy of Sciences & Humanities, 1983

"The genitalia were little noted by early authors . . . the female genitalia being completely disregarded. . . ." (Publisher's catalogue.)

The Ferns of Minnesota
Rolla Tryon
Minneapolis, Minn.: University of Minnesota Press, 1954

Mushrooms of Idaho
Edmund E. Tylutki
Moscow, Id.: University Press of Idaho, 1979

On the Composition of a Mangold-wurzel Kept for Two Years
Dr Augustus Voelcker
Printed by W. Clowes and Sons, 1859

Entomology in Sport
Hon. Mary Ward and Lady Jane Mahon
Paul Jerrard & Son, c. 1859

Teach Your Chicken to Fly Manual
Trevor Weekes
Sydney: Kangaroo Press, 1983

The Treatment of Horses by Acupuncture
Erwin Westermayer
Holsworthy: Health Science Press, 1979

The Longevity of Starved Cockroaches
Edwin R. Willis and Norman Lewis
Reprinted from The Journal of Economic Entomology, *1957*

Spider Communication
Peter N. Witt and Jerome S. Rovner (eds.)
Princeton, NJ: Princeton University Press, 1982

In Sickness and in Health

Medical oddities and sick titles

History of Dentistry in Oregon
W. Claude Adams
Portland, Oreg.: Binfords & Mort, 1956

Exposure and Removal of the Brain
E. K. Adrian, Jr
Health Series Consortium, 1984

Mechanical Exercise A Means of Cure,
Being a Description of the Zander Institute, London: Its History, Appliances,
Scope and Object. Edited by the Medical Officer to the Institution
Anon.
J. & A. Churchill, 1883

An astonishing collection of machines designed to exercise one part of the body at a time, including "Abduction" of the legs.

D 1.

D 20.

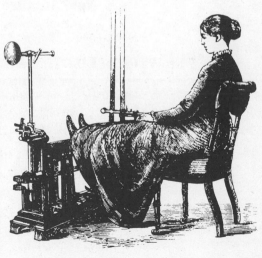

' *CHEST-EXPANDER.*' (*Passive.*)   *VIBRATING MACHINE.* (*Passive.*)

A steam-driven chest expander and a foot and leg vibrator from Mechanical Exercise A Means of Cure.

Onania;
or, The Heinous Sin of Self-Pollution, and all its Frightful Consequences, in Both Sexes, Considered
Anon.

The Author, 1725; 1759 (19th edition)

A Pictorial Book of Tongue Coating
Anon.

Kyoto: Yukonsha Publishing Co., 1981

From the publishers who brought us *A Complete Work of Acupuncture and Moxibustion* (25 vols.), we welcome this timely guide to the ancient Chinese method of diagnosis by examination of the tongue. To Western eyes, unfamiliar with this technique, the 257 coloured photographs of people sticking their tongues out may seem unusual – rude, even. But note the sheer poetry of captions such as:

11: Whitish tongue with a thin whitish moist slippery fur

25: Whitish tongue with reddened tip and thick yellowish white greasy fur

63: Pink tongue with red spots, purple speckles and thin whitish greasy fur

139: Dull red furless tongue with scanty slobber

196: Deep red tongue with a slippery moist "mouldy sauce paste" fur

217: Bluish purple lean small tongue with a white rotten fur

A Short Account of the Origin, Progress and Present State of the New Rupture Society
Anon.

"Published by the Society", S. Gosnell, Printer, 1816

The Water of Life. A Treatise on Urine-therapy*
John W. Armstrong

True Health Publishing Co., 1949

(*The Indian edition is euphemistically listed in *Indian Books in Print* as "Wine therapy".)

On the Writing of the Insane
George Mackenzie Bacon

J. Churchill & Sons, 1870

A Government Committee of Enquiry on the Light Metal Artificial Leg
Captain Henry Hume Chisholm Baird

n.p., 1923

The Desoutter Artificial Leg is particularly recommended, and Part 3 of the book gives the records achieved with the aid of this new marvel: e.g. London to Brighton in 15 hours 21 minutes by Mr Bell, thus beating his previous record on another make of metal leg by 4 hours 29 minutes.

How to Stop Your Toddler from Driving You Crazy
Linda Bairstow
Port Washington, NY: Ashley Books, 1984

Old Age: Its Cause and Prevention
Sanford Bennett
New York: Physical Culture Publishing Co., 1912

The electric face mask recommended "is wonderfully effective and it certainly does whiten the skin and generally improve the complexion. If accurately fitted it will last a life time" – however long that might be. "Any purchaser will get $1.50 off Macfadden's *Encyclopaedia of Physical Culture*" (see *Lust*, page 87). Bennett was also the author of *Exercising in Bed* (New York: Physical Culture Publishing Co., 1910).

Face Mask with Electric Battery   **Attachment of Face Mask**

From Old Age: Its Cause and Prevention. *Sanford Bennett's method of maintaining a youthful complexion provides a hideous alternative to maturing gracefully.*

A Comparative View of the More Intimate Nature of Fever
James Black
Longman & Co., 1826

The Romance of Proctology
Charles Elton Blanchard
Youngstown, Ohio: Medical Success Press, 1938

Brodie's Medical Work on Virility
R. J. Brodie & Co.
The Authors, n.d. (c. 1844)
Required reading before progressing to:

The Secret Companion, a Medical Work on Onanism
The Authors, 1845

Dentologia: A Poem on the Diseases of the Teeth and Their Proper Remedies
Solyman Brown
New York: American Library of Dental Science, 1840

❛On a subject so unpromising, I think all would agree with me in saying that the author has succeeded beyond all reasonable expectations. . . .

> One common destiny awaits our kind; –
> 'Tis this, that long before the infant mind
> Attains maturity – and ere the sun
> Has through the first septenniel circle run,
> The teeth, deciduous, totter and decay,
> And prompt successors hurry them away. . . .
>
> Be watchful, ye – whose fond maternal arm
> Would shield defenceless infancy from harm,
> Mark well the hour when nature's rights demand
> The skilful practice of the dentist's hand. . . .
>
> Derangement, pain and swift decay,
> Obtain in man their desolating sway,
> Corrupt his blood, infect his vital breath,
> And urge him headlong to the shades of death.❜

For the promotion of healthy teeth, the author recommends Armenian bole powder, prepared chalk, Peruvian bark and dental floss.

Colon Cleanse the Easy Way!
Vena Burnett and Jennifer Weiss
New York: n.p., c. 1979

Burr Identification System of Breast Analysis
Timothy Burr
Trenton, NJ: Hercules Publishing Co., 1965

This book is described as a scientific method of showing "why and how women's breasts reveal their character", and includes "a uniquely valuable dictionary—commentary on a thousand ways to describe women".

Fresh Air and How to Use It
Thomas Spees Carrington
New York: The National Association for the Study and Prevention of Tuberculosis, 1912

Shut Your Mouth and Save Your Life
George Catlin
N. Trübner & Co., 1869
and:

The Breath of Life; or, Mal-respiration and Its Effects Upon the Enjoyment and Life of Man
New York: John Wiley, 1861

Surplus Fat
William Francis Christie
Heinemann, 1927

Cluthe's Advice to the Ruptured
Charles Cluthe
Bloomfield, NJ: Chas. Cluthe & Sons (of the Cluthe Rupture Institute), 1915 (71st edition)

Quickly Cured, but Would Feel Lost Without It. "Your truss cured me in about six months but as I feel lost without it, I am still wearing it. . . ." John J. Glaser, Lancaster, Ohio.

CLUTHE'S ADVICE
TO THE RUPTURED

71st Edition

BY

Chas. Cluthe & Sons

CLUTHE RUPTURE INSTITUTE
Bloomfield, New Jersey
(A Suburb of New York City)

Mr Cluthe's advice in a nutshell: "Buy one of my trusses".

Cancer: Is the Dog the Cause?
Samuel Walter Cort
John Bale, Sons & Danielsson, 1933

'He that keepeth a dog in domestication breaketh a fundamental law and shall not know health . . . to keep a dog, to cuddle, fondle, stroke, kiss or be kissed by a dog, is to invite disease and death.'

And it is not just cancer: the dog is also the prime cause of measles, new flu, tetanus, cerebrospinal meningitis, diphtheria, and foot-and-mouth disease.

'which shall survive, DOGANITY or HUMANITY?'

Brought to you by the publishers of *The True Nature and Mechanics of Consciousness*; *Flatfoot: The True Nature, Cause and Rational Cure*; *The Sanity of Hamlet*; *The Rat: A World Menace* and Ethelbert Blatter's *Beautiful Flowers of Kashmir*.

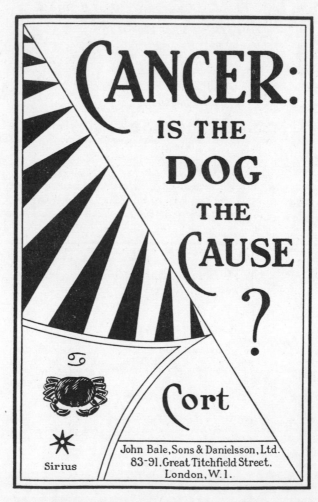

Samuel Walter Cort in a cul-de-sac of medical research.

Notes Sur la Sodomie
Jean Paul Henry Coutagne*
Lyon: H. Georg, 1880
(*Also author of *Les Drames Musicaux de Richard Wagner* (Lyons: Académie des Sciences, 1892).)

Eleven Years a Drunkard; or, The Life of Thomas Doner, Having Lost Both Arms Through Intemperance, He Wrote This Book with His Teeth As a Warning to Others
Thomas Doner
Sycamore, Ill.: Arnold Bros., 1878

How To Be Plump
Thomas Cation Duncan
Chicago, Ill.: Duncan Bros., 1878

On the Conditions Under which Leprosy Has Declined in Iceland*
Edward H. Ehlers
National Leprosy Fund and Macmillan, 1895
(*Prize Essays on Subjects Connected with Leprosy, 6 vols., 1895–7, Vol. 2.)

The Unfailing Efficacy of Medical Electricity
in Imparting Health, Strength and Durable Vigour to Enfeebled Organs and Functions Whether the Result of Natural Causes, Imprudences in Early Life or in Mature Age, by Means of the Electro-Galvanic Improved Patent Self-Adjusting Curative Appliance, or Ne Plus Ultra, &c.
Dr Lionel Elliott*
The Author, 1868
(*"Author of the Popular Work on *The Complete and Permanent Cure of Spermatorrhoea, Syphilis, Gonorrhoea, Gleet, Stricture, &c., and the Granulation and Cicatrization of Ulcers and Deep Seated Wounds &c. &c.*")

A Treatise on the Stomach and Its Trials
James Crossley Eno*
Leeds: Newbery & Sons, 1881 (11th edition)
(*His only published work.)

‘Yes; when I suffer from a brain overwrought –
Excited, feverish, worn, from laboured thought –
Harassed by anxious care, or sudden grief,
I run to Eno and obtain relief.’

New National Strength Through Beauty of the Teeth
Henry C. Ferris
New York: The Author, 1919

Jogging – The Dance of Death
Robert Gene Fineberg
Port Washington, NY: Ashley Books, 1984
Ashley Books also publish Wassersug's *JARM – Jogging with Yours Arms to Live Longer* (see page 96).

The History of Cold Bathing
Sir John Floyer
S. Smith & B. Walford, 1706
Sir John was a great advocate of the cold dip and wrote several works on the subject. However, even he realized it was not always the right remedy:

❝ A Gentleman of the Temple, a hale man, of a strong athletick Habit . . . stayed in the cold bath of Mr Baynes at least 15 minutes . . . but it so chill'd him, that he had much ado to recover it, and was not well in some time. . . . ❞

Syphilis; or, A Poetical History of the French Disease
English edition (trans. N. Tate)
For Jacob Tonson, 1686
The English translation of Girolamo Fracastoro's *Syphilis sive morbus Gallicus* (Verona: n.p., 1530) – the book that gave us the word "syphilis".

Spiritual Midwifery
Ina May Gaskin
Summertown, Tenn.: The Book Publishing Co., 1978

The Hive; or, Mental Gatherings. For the Benefit of the Idiot and His Institution
Eliza Grove
Earlswood: The Asylum for Idiots, 1857

Fingernail Biting: Theory, Research and Treatment
H. H. Hadley
Lancaster: MTP Press Ltd, 1983

The Serious Lesson in President Harding's Case of Gonorrhoea
Julius E. Haldeman
Girard, Ka.: Haldeman-Julius, "A Little Blue Book No. 1580", 1931

Fish's Schizophrenia
Max Hamilton
Bath: John Wright, 1984

The Handbook for Fitters of Camp Supports. With Anatomical Drawings by Tom Jones
Rhoda Grace Hendrick
Jackson, Mich.: S. H. Camp & Co., 1938

Scurvy: Past and Present

Alfred F. Hess

Academic Press, 1982

The Culture of the Abdomen, the Cure of Obesity and Constipation

F. A. Hornibrook

Heinemann, 1924

A classic that went to eleven editions between 1924 and 1937, cured Arnold Bennett of dyspepsia and gave H. G. Wells "a new lease of life".

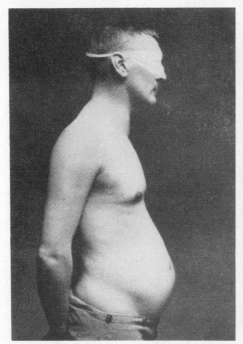

FIG. 17.—Here we see a man of early middle life whose abdomen has become pendulous and protuberant, due to excessive local fat deposit and faulty posture.

FIG. 18. —Shows the same subject after a course of treatment. Note the striking change in general contour and condition.

A masked man – probably not H. G. Wells – from The Culture of the Abdomen, *showing the* trompe l'oeil *effect of wearing outsize trousers.*

Practical Infectious Diseases

Richard D. Meyer

New York: John Wiley & Sons, 1983

Bournemouth in Lung Troubles
Vincent Milner
Baillière, Tindall & Cox, 1896
Intended to promote the town as a centre for the alleviation of diseases of the air-passages. The first owner of the authors' copy of this book apparently didn't make it to the south coast, as the phlegm-stained cover clearly testifies.

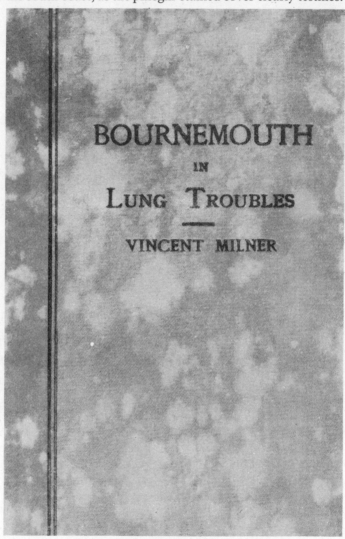

The last resort for those with breathing problems.

Art of Prolonging One's Life
Christoph Wilhelm Von Hufeland
J. Bell, 1797

Amputation Stumps: Their Care and After-treatment
Sir Godfrey Martin Huggins
Henry Froude, 1918

De l'Amputation du Pénis
Louis Jullien
Paris: n.p., 1873

You Can't Catch Diabetes from a Friend
Lynne Kipnis and Susan Adler
Gainsville, Fla.: Triad, 1979

Coma Arousal
Edward B. Le Winn
New York: Doubleday, 1985
"No special equipment or expertise is necessary". (Publisher's catalogue.)

The Fountain of Youth;
or, Curing by Water. How You May Quickly Overcome Acute and Chronic Illness by the Use of the Biological Blood-Washing Bath. With an Introduction by Bernarr Macfadden
Dr Benedict Lust
New York: Macfadden Publications, 1923

Bernarr Macfadden* (no stranger to quack medicine, as students of the subject will know) refers in his introduction to the unfortunately named Dr Lust's "profound interest in Mr Christos Parasco's discovery" – a discovery which "actually washes the poisons from the system". The "Technique of Rectal Irrigation" in "The Knee–Chest Position" is apparently best, "allowing from four to six pints of water

Leading rectal irrigators Parasco and Lust pose unselfconsciously for the frontispiece photograph of their Meisterwerk *– but thankfully rely on line drawings to depict their techniques.*

to be injected safely and without inconvenience". Pure water, mind; do not use soap-suds, soda or salt. He concludes:

‘Ponce de Léon may have been wrong in the notion that he could, perhaps, make his body live forever . . . but he was quite right in thinking that, when all was said and done, what he and the rest of the human race needed was a Bath.’

(*Author of *Vitality Supreme for Men and Women*; *The Real Secret of Keeping Young*; the five-volume *Macfadden Encyclopaedia of Physical Culture*; *Manhood and Marriage*; *Strengthening the Eyes*; *Gaining Weight* and *How to Reduce Weight*.)

From the top of the head to the base of the spine may be showered in this position, though the greatest effect will be secured upon the upper half of the trunk, the shoulders and neck. This is an excellent position if there is dizziness or other disturbance while lying face down. The latter position, however, will permit of greater relaxation, which is a valuable part of the treatment.

While this position can, in many cases, be held for a short time only, it shows a superior method for reaching the external pelvic organs, lower abdomen, inner surfaces of the thighs and the perineum—all closely associated with the sexual function and the health of the inner pelvic organs. After a few moments in this position the patient may assume the next position for a continuation to some extent of the same effect.

Rejuvenation by showering: two of the 69 positions illustrated in Lust's Fountain of Youth.

The Romance of
Leprosy

BY
E. MACKERCHAR, L.L.A.

The Romance of Leprosy
E. Mackerchar
The Mission to Lepers, 1949

"Romance" and "leprosy" do not come easily in the same breath – except to Mr Mackerchar. And even he, intrepid enthusiast that he is, realizes that "even the intrepid enthusiast must falter on the threshold of such service". Nothing daunted, the author plunges into his subject with alacrity:

> ❢All down the ages the disease of leprosy has fascinated writer, artist, and poet, providing each in turn with themes upon which to exercise the loftiest imagination, and the highest artistic skill.❜

The heights of romance are to be found in the brief biography of Mrs Gong, the Chinese bible-woman of Foochow:

> ❢Without the least fear of the disease this intrepid worker threw her whole soul and strength into the task allotted to her . . . the warning to avoid close contact with those to whom she ministered fell on deaf ears. . . . Nine years passed and then the blow fell. . . . "I never thought I would get it", was the pathetic remark of this brave sufferer . . . her passing left a blank which it was almost impossible to fill.❜

Grow Your Own Hair
Ron MacLaren
Glasgow: Heathway Publications, 1947

Living Canvas: a Romance of Aesthetic Surgery
Elisabeth Margetson*
Methuen, 1936

(*Known mainly for her Ward Lock novels: *Women are Different* (1936), *A Kiss for a Sailor* (1943), *Cancel All Our Vows* (1944) and *Better to Marry* (1946).)

A Study of Masturbation and Its Reputed Sequelae
John Francis William Meagher
Baillière, Tindall & Cox, 1924

An enlightened approach – "Any recommendation to marry in order to cure the habit is abominably bad and unfair". The title was altered for the second edition to *A Study of Masturbation and the Psychosexual Life* (1929).

89

Troubles We Don't Talk About*
Joseph Franklin Montague
Philadelphia, Pa.: J. B. Lippincott Co., 1927
(*Diseases of the rectum.)
Also author of:

Why Bring That Up? A Guide To and From Seasickness
New York: The Home Health Library, 1936

WHY BRING THAT UP?

A Guide to and from Seasickness

By

DR. J. F. MONTAGUE

Medical Director, New York Intestinal Sanitarium; Late of University and
Bellevue Hospital Medical College; Fellow American Medical
Association; Fellow New York Academy of Sciences;
Fellow New York Pathological Society; Sometime
Fellow New York Academy of Medicine
and American College of Surgeons.

Editor of
HEALTH DIGEST

"There's a cure for every ill"

THE HOME HEALTH LIBRARY INC.
516 FIFTH AVENUE
NEW YORK

Dr Montague suggests ways of keeping it down.

Guts

John Edward Morton

Baltimore, Md.: University Park Press, 1979

Electricity as a Cause of Cholera, or Other Epidemics, etc.

Sir James Murray

Dublin: J. M'Glashan, 1849

The Ethics of Medical Homicide and Mutilation

Austin O'Malley

New York: The Devin-Adair Co., 1922

De la Prolongation de la Vie Humaine par le Café

H. Petit

Paris: J. B. Baillière, 1862

A Treatise on the Virtues and Efficacy of the Saliva, or Fasting Spittle,

Being Conveyed into the Intestines by Eating a Crust of Bread, Early in a Morning Fasting, in Relieving the Gout, Scurvey [*sic*], Gravel, Stone, Rheumatism, &c, Arising from Obstructions: Also, on the Great Cures Accomplished by the Fasting Spittle, When Externally Applied to Recent Cuts, Sore Eyes, Corns, Warts &c.

"A Physician"

Salem, Mass.: Henry Whipple, 1844 (1st American edition taken from 10th London edition)

The Dentist in Art

Jens Jorgen Pindborg and L. Marvitz

George Proffer, 1961

The Mesmeric Guide for Family Use

S. D. Saunders

H. Baillière, 1852

How to cure all diseases by hypnotizing your spouse, children, etc. Its fifty pages give concise instructions on curing deafness, cancer, consumption and the common cold.

Why Aluminium Pans Are Dangerous

Edgar J. Saxon

C. W. Daniel, 1939

Backache and Figure Relief by Self-Revolving Hipbones

William Schoenau

Los Angeles, Calif.: The Author, 1951

Printed on the title-page is the legend: "The words herein are all defined in Webster's Dictionary".

I Knew 3,000 Lunatics
Victor Robert Small
New York: Farrar & Rinehart, 1935; Rich & Cowan, 1935

'I was privileged by fate and fortune to view from many angles the enactment of a complex drama of romance and comic pathos, and dark tragedy . . . and the theater wherein this drama was being enacted was an asylum for the insane; and the actors were the 3,000 lunatics confined therein . . . for six years I watched this show.'

Ironically, in 1938 this real-life drama was made into a play by Hardie Albright – who dropped its snappy title in favour of *All the Living*.

By VICTOR R. SMALL, M.D.

I KNEW
3000 LUNATICS

LONDON
RICH & COWAN, LTD.
25 SOHO SQUARE, W. 1

How to Get Fat
Edward Smith
John Smith & Co., 1865

Injurious Effects of the Constant Use of Baby Carriages and Bicycles on the Physical Development of the Young
Henry Hollingsworth Smith
Philadelphia, Pa.: n.p., 1881

Nasal Maintenance: Nursing Your Nose Through Troubled Times
William Alan Stuart
New York: McGraw-Hill, 1983

An Essay on Diseases Incidental to Literary and Sedentary Persons
Samuel Auguste André David Tissot
Printed for Edward and Charles Dilly, 1768

'It is universally known that there are books compos'd without any strength of genius, which appear quite insipid and unaffecting to the reader and only tire the eyes; but those that are compos'd with an exquisite force of ideas, and with an exact connexion of thought, elevate the soul, and fatigue it with the very pleasure which, the more compleat, lasting, and frequent it is, breaks the man the more. . . . There is still living at Paris a professor of Rhetoric who fainted away whilst he was perusing some of the sublime passages of Homer. The head itself, and the nerves, and the stomach which is fuller of nerves than any other part, first suffer for the errors of the mind. . . .

Peter Jurieu [who] was formerly famous for . . . his labours in writing books of controversy, and expounding the apocalypse, so disorder'd his brain, that though he thought like a man in other respects, he was firmly persuaded that the seven fits of cholic with which he was tormented, had been occasioned by a constant fight between seven horsemen that were shut up in his bowels. . . .

Strong and illustrious sons are seldom the offspring of illustrious men . . . whilst the mind of the father was entirely given up to meditation, and his corporeal functions totally neglected, the vivifying liquor was perhaps defrauded of that part of elaboration which it should have had from the brain, so as to give a proper tone to the embryo. . . .'

As the author summarizes, "It is dangerous to break upon rocks of too great learning".

New Views on Baldness
Henry Paul Truefitt
n.p., 1863

Crook Frightfulness

"A Victim"

Birmingham: Cornish, 1932; Birmingham: Moody Bros., 1935 (revised edition)

The author of this book, identified only as "A Victim", recounts the story of his life as a rent collector in the East End of London, in New Zealand and in the West Indies. Ordinary stuff, you might think, but *Crook Frightfulness* is the autobiography of a hunted man who believes himself to be continually hounded and molested by evil men, or "crooks".

A sampling of reviews gives some indication of how this unique work was received. *The Lancet* (12 October 1935) called it a "painful narrative . . . an account of the persecution to which its author believes himself to have been subjected since 1922 by powerful and ubiquitous enemies. . . . Few such detailed first-hand accounts as this have been published." "Fidelio", reviewing it in the *Border Telegraph* (31 December 1935) described it as "one of the most extraordinary books I have read for many years." The *Glasgow Evening News* (28 December 1935), however, refers principally to the author's warning concerning the monotony of his subject, which it describes as "well founded".

Indeed, it is hard to view this book as anything but the ravings of a paranoid suffering from delusions of persecution. But in chapters with titles like "I am a marked man" and "The underworld wants me", there is pathos. Describing how he accepted the job of rent collector in a "tough" part of London, he writes:

> How was I to know that I had of my own volition opened the doors of Hell — to turn me from a cheery, care-free youth of 18 to a prematurely aged man, terrified by horrible men, threatening my sanity and life?

His persecution is far from commonplace. He was threatened physically and mentally by gangs of thugs wherever he travelled — the inhabitants of the West Indies, for example, seem almost to be waiting for him to arrive so that they can start attacking him. He is also "molested" in various unique ways: "I have had experiences which suggest crooks sometimes use a stethoscope apparatus which enables them to hear your thoughts." He also provides a detailed account of what he describes as "ventriloquial terrorism" whereby

> a molestor using ventriloquism may be in a house or building or walking along in a tram or 'bus or in a car, yet he can throw his voice anywhere undetected by those who are near them.

This technique gives rise to various embarrassing experiences, including one where

> I had just bidden adieu to a friend on the Aberystwyth Marine Parade and had just turned away from him when I heard the words — "The old sod" — said in my voice tones too! There was no one else near us two and my friend probably thought I had said these insulting terms. Of course, a ventriloquial crook had done this trick as a trying molest to me.

The author goes on to describe how he attempted to get Scotland Yard on the trail of the "crooks" and "ventriloquial terrorists", but for some reason they would not take him seriously.

Crook Frightfulness

(REVISED)

By a Victim

They are the most powerful, terrible and pitiless killers, cunning, amazingly and enormously treacherous.

The serpent . . . more subtle than any.
Genesis iii. 1.

MOODY BROTHERS, LTD.
34, LIVERY STREET,
BIRMINGHAM, ENGLAND.

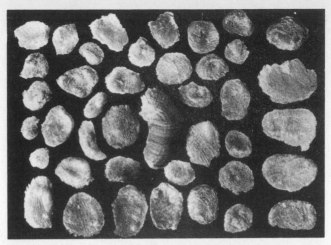

A typical page from the catalogue of the Felix Wagner Callosity Collection.

A Handbook of "Chiropody"
Giving the Causes and Treatment of Corns, Callosities, Bunions, Chilblains and the Diseases of the Toe-nails
Felix Wagner
Osborne, Garrett & Co., 1903

An excellent little work on the diseases of the feet, "intended to direct attention to the much neglected art of Chiropody".

Extracted callosities and deformed big toes are to Mr Wagner what stamps are to the philatelist, and the book is lavishly illustrated with mounted examples from his collection.

JARM – How to Jog with Your Arms to Live Longer
Joseph D. Wassersug
Port Washington, NY: Ashley Books, 1983

In a blatant attempt to cover all possible markets, Ashley Books are also the publishers of Fineberg's *Jogging – The Dance of Death* (see page 84).

The Strange Story of False Teeth
John Woodforde
Routledge & Kegan Paul, 1968

The authors have in their collection a copy of a "Special edition presented by Reckitt & Sons Ltd., manufacturers of Steradent".

How We Catch Cold
Thomas Giordani Wright
J. & A. Churchill, 1881

The Diagnosis of the Acute Abdomen in Rhyme
"Zeta"*
H. K. Lewis, 1947
(*The pseudonym of Sir Vincent Zachary Cope.)

Love, Marriage and. . . .
Encounters exotic and erotic

Seven Wives and Seven Prisons; or, Experiences in the Life of a Matrimonial Monomaniac. A True Story Written by Himself
L. A. Abbott

New York: The Author, 1870

The frontispiece portrait is of "My first and worst wife".

Love, Woman, Marriage: the Grand Secret
Anon.

Boston, Mass.: Randolph Publishing Co., 1872

'No description, critique, or synopsis can do justice to this mighty work, which ought to be bound in gold and be on the table of every man, woman and youth in the land and in the world. It is an exhaustive and large work.' (Publisher's description.)

MY FIRST AND WORST WIFE

Literature of Kissing
Charles C. Bombaugh
Philadelphia, Pa. and London: J. B. Lippincott, 1876
Extracts from this original anthology of kissography – now sadly superseded by the commercial "kissagram":

> ❛Who was it caught me when I fell
> And Kissed the place to make it well?
> My mother.
>
> Catch the white-handed nymphs in shady places,
> And woo sweet kisses from averted faces
>
> The overture kiss to the opera of love.
>
> Life's autumnal blossoms fall
> And death's brown clinging lips impress
> The long cold kiss that waits us all.❜

Orgasmus und Super-Orgasmus
Ruediger Bosschmann
Flensburg: Stephenson Verlag, 1972
and:

Sex + Sex = Gruppensex
Flensburg: Stephenson Verlag, 1970

Is the Pleasure Worth the Penalty? A Common-sense View of the Leading Vice of the Age
Henry Butter
Job Caudwell, 1866

How to Speak and Write to Girls for Friendship
B. A. Chinaka
Onitsha: Njoku & Sons Bookshop, c. 1963

Traps for the Young
Anthony Comstock
New York: Funk & Wagnalls, 1883
A spotter's guide to enable the confiscation of "immoral literature" before it gets into the wrong hands.

Women Around Hitler
Randolph S. Davies
E. Newman, Know Thine Enemy *series, c. 1943*
"This is a real thriller. It is a story which recalls mediaeval life, loves, intrigues and murders in the dark passages of castles ... well illustrated [i.e.: one drawing]." (Publisher's description.)

A threepenny thrill exposing Hitler's inadequacies.

"One of his women, when asked why her friendship with Hitler came to an end, said that she had had a disappointment with him which did not redound to his advantage."

How to Pick Up Women in Discos
Don Diebel
Houston, Tex.: Gemini Publishing Co., 1981

The Girdle of Chastity
Eric John Dingwall
George Routledge & Sons, 1931
The definitive book on chastity belts.

Sexual Behaviour of the American Women
Govind Sadasiva Ghuyre
Bombay: Thacker, 1975

Wife Battering: a Systems Theory Approach
Jean Giles-Sims
Guilford Press, 1983

How To Be Happy Though Married
E. J. Hardy
T. Fisher Unwin, 1885

'To those brave men and women who have ventured, or intend to venture, into that state which is "a blessing to a few, a curse to many, and a great uncertainty to all", this book is dedicated in admiration of their courage.'

Wed To a Lunatic. A Wild, Weird Yarn of Love and Some Other Things Delivered in the Form of Hash for the Benefit of Tired Readers
Frank Warren Hastings*
St Johnsbury, Vt.: L. W. Rowell, 1896

2nd edition:
Wed To a Lunatic. A Lie.
St Johnsbury, Vt.: The Caledonian Press, 1901
"enlarged and revised to meet the requirements of modern science"
(*"Author of several widely unknown works.")

How to Love Every Minute of Your Life
Gay Hendricks and Carol Leavenworth
Englewood Cliffs, NJ: Prentice-Hall, 1978

How to Forgive Your Ex-husband
Marcia Hootman and Patt Perkins
New York: Doubleday, 1983

The White Women's Protective Ordinance: Sexual Anxiety and Politics in Papua
Amirah Inglis
Sussex University and Chatto & Windus, 1975

Training of the Young in Laws of Sex
Hon. Edward Lyttleton
Longman, 1900

The obtuseness of this guide for parents suggests that final guidance to the child would be so vague as to be meaningless.

"Strength of appetite" in a child of ten or eleven suggests, according to the author, that "physical temptation later will be very strong". This is the only sure symptom that a boy is "contracting the habit" of "this particular foe". Lyttleton was also the author of *The Causes and Prevention of Immorality in Schools* (The Social Purity Alliance, 1887).

Sex Instruction for Irish Farmers
Charles McSherry
Dublin: Mercier Press, 1980

Although listed in the "humour" section of the Mercier Press catalogue, the British Library certainly takes this one seriously. It is locked away and can be read only at a special desk reserved for "Readers Using Special Books" (i.e. pornography).

> ‘The subject will no doubt evoke some curiosity in the mind of the discerning reader. . . .
>
> Why should the Irish Farmer be singled out for special attention? . . . It will be seen that the needs of the barman from Blackrock and the farmer from Faslcarragh are poles apart. . . . We need more Bachelors of Agriculture and less agricultural bachelors. . . .’

The book fails to raise many laughs, so maybe the publishers have miscatalogued it; they could have a valuable textbook on their hands. . . .

Men Loving Themselves: Images of Male Self-sexuality
Jack Morin
Burlingame, Calif.: Down There Press, 1980

"Sensitive photographs of twelve men doing what they usually do to pleasure themselves." (Publisher's catalogue.)

The Romance of Lust; or, Early Expressions
William S. Potter
n.p., 1873–6 (4 vols.)

The Sex Practitioner: a Step by Step Guide to the Pleasures of Sex
Harry Prick
New York: I. M. Horny, 1945

According to the National Union Catalog, there is only one recorded copy of this title (in the library of the University of Oregon, Eugene). Or could it possibly be a librarian's spoof?

Sex Life of the Foot and Shoe
William A. Rossi
New York: Saturday Review Press, 1976; Routledge & Kegan Paul, 1977

Teach Yourself Sex
William Ewart Sargent
English Universities Press, 1951

The Causes of Infidelity Removed
Revd Stephen Smith
Utica, NY: Grosh & Hutchinson, 1839

The One-Minute Lover
Minnie Weiner and Zazu Putz*
New York: New American Library, 1983
(*"Putz" is Yiddish for "penis".)

12
Deviant Diversions
Peculiar pastimes

What people do in their spare time has excited many writers. There is a vast range of subjects from which to draw, but here we have concentrated on leisure activities, cooking and travel.

Leisure Activities

How to Boil Water in a Paper Bag
Anon.
n.p., 1891

How to Eat a Peanut
Anon.
New York?: n.p., c. 1900

How to Twirl a Baton
Anon.
Chicago, Ill.: Ludwig & Ludwig, c. 1930

How to Vamp Without Music
Anon.
J. E. Dallas, 1943

How to Walk
Anon.
Evening News, 1903

Magic in India
Anon.
Edinburgh: n.p., 1852
With an illustration of a snake-charmer whistling *Auld Lang Syne*.

Ten Good Tricks With Empty Bass Bottles
Anon.
Burton-on-Trent: Bass Ltd, 1929

The Great Pantyhose Crafts Book
Ed and Stevie Baldwin
New York: Western Publishing Co., Inc., 1982

This apparently quite genuine (i.e. it wasn't meant to be funny) book gives patterns for forty different articles that can be made from old tights, starting with "gifts and bazaar [*sic*] items for everyone".

The authors' list of items borders on the grotesque:

❛Little Black Evening Bag – If you've always admired the evening purses in the stores but hated to spend the money, then this project is for you!❜

"The perfect touch . . . for your home decor" can be created in the shape of a life-size stuffed "granny", and "shady lady", while the pantyhose cactus "is sure to be a conversation piece" and "requires even less care than a real one". And for that "sparkling addition to a special occasion" the Thanksgiving Turkey will be "a decorative addition to your Thanksgiving table – or tuck a brick inside and use him as a unique door stop".

Readers of this husband-and-wife team's first bestseller will thrill to their latest outpouring: *More Great Pantyhose Crafts: Recycle Old Pantyhose into Dolls, Wall Hangings, Musical Boxes, Holiday Decorations, and Much More* (New York: Doubleday, 1985).

"Granny" & "Shady Lady"

These incredibly life-like characters may be the most enjoyable projects you have ever made. If you place them in a chair in your living room, they will watch over your home when you are not there, and may possibly scare off any uninvited guests.

The ultimate deterrents – both made from old tights.

Master Pieces: Making Furniture from Paintings
Richard Ball and Peter Campbell
Poole: Blandford, 1983

Painting and Drawing Water
Norman Battershill
A. & C. Black, 1984

Practical Taxidermy and Home Decoration
Joseph H. Batty
New York: Orange Judd, 1880

Inkle Weaving
Lavinia Bradley
Routledge & Kegan Paul, 1982

Dinkum Magic
J. Albert Briggs
Alexandria, New South Wales: The Austral Magic Co., 1928

How to Make Your Own Woodcarving Tools from Nails, Hacksaw Blades and Umbrella Ribs
Jack Van Deckter
New York: Venturecraft Kits Co., 1984

In Love and Unity. A Book About Brushmaking
Thomas Girtin
Hutchinson, 1961

Teach Yourself Alcoholism
Meier Glatt
Teach Yourself Books, 1975

Let's Make Some Undies*
Marion Hall
W. Foulsham & Co., 1954
(*In the *Let's Make It* series.)

Government-surplus parachutes see further active service.

The Art of Chapeaugraphy
John G. Hamley
G. Routledge, 1923
The long-awaited sequel to:
Chapeaugraphy; or, Twenty-Five Heads Under One Hat
W. & F. Hamley, c. 1885

The Mystery of Golf
Theodore Arnold Haultain
New York: Macmillan, 1910

Side and Screw, Being Notes on the Theory and Practise of the Game of Billiards
Charles Dealtry Locock
Longmans, 1901

The Irish Literary Quiz Book
Paddy Lysaght
Dingle, Co. Kerry: Brandon Books, 1984

The Unwritten Laws of Fox-Hunting. Notes on the Use of the Horn and the Whistle, and List of 5,000 Names of Hounds
C. F. P. McNeill
Vinton & Co., 1911

Levitation for Terrestrials
Robert Kingley Morison (ed.)
Ascent, 1977

The Projection of the Astral Body
Sylvan Joseph Muldoon and Hereward Carrington
Rider & Co., 1929

Searching for Railway Telegraph Insulators
W. Keith Neal
St Saviours, Guernsey: The Signal Box Press, 1982

Jerks In From Short Leg
"Quid"*
Harrison, 1866
(*Pseudonym – probably Robert Allan Fitzgerald.)

Build Your Own Hindenburg
Alan Rose
New York: Putnam, 1983

"Be Prepared": the oldest boy scout in the movement, the aptly named Mr Pinkney – author of Rope Spinning *– (seen here in his official Baden-Powell waffle-top socks), demonstrates his technique for committing suicide in a rhododendron bush. Or could he be a devotee of Prout's* Scouts in Bondage *(see page 10)?*

Rope Spinning
D. W. Pinkney
Herbert Jenkins, 1930

The Passionate Game: Lessons in Chess and Love
Gustav Schenk
G. Routledge & Son, 1937
The first principles of chess as explained in a series of love-letters – or is it the other way round?

Fun on the Billiard Table
"Stancliffe"
C. Arthur Pearson, 1899
From the author who brought us:

The Autobiography of a Caddy-Bag
Methuen, 1924

Dyeing Wool with Fungi
Carla and Erik Sundstrom
Stockholm: ICA Bokforlag, c. 1984

Spirit Rapping Made Easy
Dion Sweird
Felix McGlennan, 1926
This basic textbook is designed to ensure a medium level of success.

A poltergeist doing George Formby impressions.

Folding Table Napkins
Mariane Van Borstedt and Ulla Prytz
Sweden: ICA Forlaget, 1968; Sterling Publishing Co., Little Craft series, 1972

Fun with Knotting String
Heidy Willsmore
Kaye & Ward, 1977

Cooking the Books

Les Gourmets au Congo
Anon.
Antwerp: J. E. Buschmann, n.d.

Radiation Cookery Book
Anon.
Birmingham: Radiation, 1927

Report of the Temperature Reached in Army Biscuits During Baking,
Especially with Reference to the Destruction of the Imported Flour-Moth *Ephestia Kuhniella Zeller*
Anon.
Report reprinted from the Journal of the Royal Army Medical Corps, *1913*

Some Interesting Facts about Margarine
Anon.
n.p., n.d.
Does the title suggest that certain facts about margarine are *not* interesting?

Pernicious Pork; or, Astounding Revelations of the Evil Effects of Eating Swine Flesh
William T. Hallett
New York: Broadway Publishing Co., 1903

Eat Your House: Art Eco Guide to Self-sufficiency
Frederic Hobbs
Carmel, Calif.: Virginia City Restoration Corporation, 1980

The Complete Book of Bacon
William J. Hogan
Northwood Books, 1978

The Anthropologists' Cookbook
Jessica Kuper (ed.)
New York: Universe Books, 1977
Includes a tasty roast-dog recipe from Ponape.

Cold Meat and How to Disguise It

Mrs M. E. Rattray

C. Arthur Pearson, 1904

What To Do with Cold Mutton: a Book of Réchauffés

Mary Renny*

Richard Bentley & Son, 1887

(*First published in 1863 under the pseudonym "A Gentleman of Moderate Means".)

Unmentionable Cuisine

Calvin W. Schwabe

Charlottesville, Va.: University Press of Virginia, 1979

Containing recipes for stewed cat, silk-worm omelette and red-ant chutney.

Entertaining with Insects; or, The Original Guide to Insect Cookery

Ronald L. Taylor and Barbara J. Carter (illustrated by John Gregory Tweed)

Santa Barbara, Calif.: Woodbridge Press Publishing Co., 1976

Living Without Eating

Herbert Thurston

n.p., 1931

Appealing Potatoes

Princess Weikersheim

Hutchinson, 1981

The Book of Marmalade: Its Antecedents, Its History and Its Role in the World Today

C. Anne Wilson

Constable, 1985

How to Cook Husbands

Elizabeth Strong Worthington

New York: Dodge Publishing Co., 1899

and:

The Gentle Art of Cooking Wives

New York: Dodge Publishing Co., c. 1900

How to Survive Snack Attacks Naturally

Shari and Judi Zucker

Santa Barbara, Calif.: Woodbridge Press Publishing Co., 1979

Travellers' Tales

Unprotected Females in Norway; or, The Pleasantest Way of Travelling There
Anon.*
G. Routledge & Co., 1857
and also:

Unprotected Females in Sicily, Calabria, and on the Top of Mount Aetna
Routledge, Warnes & Co., 1859
(*Probably Emily or Helen Lowe.)

Weymouth, the English Naples
Anon.
Middlesbrough: Hood & Co., 1910

❝Go to Weymouth. There you will find pure air, pure water, warm sunshine, bright sea, sweet sloping pebbly beaches, firm fine sands, good bathing, boating, yachting, cycling, golfing, etc. The distance from London is 142½ miles, and the journey takes a few minutes over three hours.❞

Any suggestion of similarity with Naples is purely ridiculous.

See Weymouth . . .

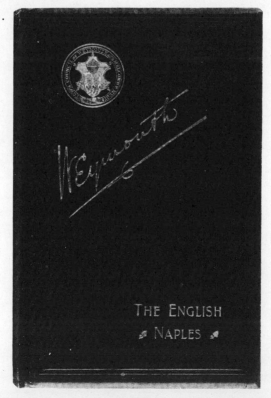

. . . and die.

112

Across Siberia on a Bicycle
Robert L. Jefferson
Cycle Press, 1896
Mr Jefferson also went:

Awheel to Moscow and Back
Sampson Low, 1895
and:

To Constantinople on a Bicycle
Cycle Press, 1895

Gay Bulgaria
Stowers Johnson
Robert Hale, 1964

Here and There in Yucatan
Alice Le Plongeon
New York: J. W. Bouton, 1886

Walking Backwards, and Other Narratives
"A.M.C."
Stirling: Drummond's Tract Depot, 1909

Malaya Upside Down
Kee-Onn Chin
Singapore: Jitts & Co., 1946

Life and Laughter 'midst the Cannibals
Clifford Whiteley Collinson
Hurst & Blackett, 1926
Relates the hilarious story of a sailor visiting the Solomon Islands who avoided being eaten by cannibals but whose false teeth fell overboard; in attempting to retrieve them, he was eaten alive by a shark.

Recollections of Squatting in Victoria
Edward Micklethwaite Curr
Melbourne: George Robertson, 1883; Carlton South: Melbourne University Press, 1965 (reprint)

Gardening in Egypt: a Handbook for Gardening in Lower Egypt
Walter Draper
Upcott Gill, 1895

‘So far as I am aware, no book on Egyptian gardening has yet been published in English. . . .’

Astray in the Forest
Edward Sylvester Ellis
Cassell & Co., 1898

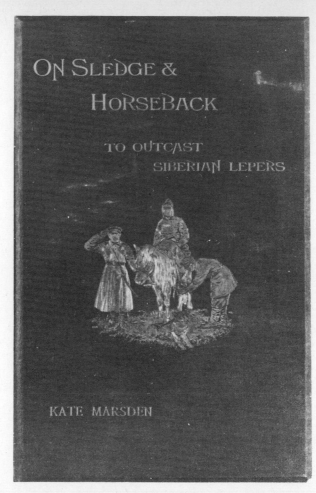

The gilt-decorated cover of Kate Marsden's account of her epic adventure.

On Sledge and Horseback to Outcast Siberian Lepers
Kate Marsden
The Record Press, 1892

This is a classic book of the "Up the Lower Mekong with Rod and Line" genre, but with a portmanteau title of such mindblowing range that it leaves the competition in its snowy wake: travel by more than one arduous method; a charitable rescue mission to untouchables; a journey to a remote and little-known land – and by a Victorian woman! All this is summarized in the title. The book itself is no less enthralling. The cover depicts the intrepid Miss Marsden embarking on her epic quest to seek out frostbitten lepers. She sits boldly, whip in hand, astride what appears to be a Shetland pony. One faithful retainer adjusts her stirrup while another lends a steadying hand to the pony's reins. In the foreground a collie either crouches or has lost its hind legs in an unfortunate encounter with an outcast Siberian canine leper.

Within the copies in the authors' collection, there is a facsimile of a black-edged letter dated 27 October 1892 from no less an address than Balmoral Castle. Signed by Henry A. Ponsonby, General Private Secretary to Queen Victoria, it declares that "The Queen has taken a deep interest in the work undertaken by Miss Marsden amongst the lepers" and requests that every possible assistance be provided to aid her work. A second letter, from the Empress of Russia, endorses this request.

The frontispiece illustration depicts "Kate Marsden in travelling dress", which consists of an ankle-length fur coat and balaclava helmet; a "map of her route" on the wall behind her zig-zags across most of Russia. There she encountered the subjects of the extraordinary pictures that embellish her book: "Destitute Leper – Taken from Life", "Hut or Hovel of Lepers", "Tent-life among the Lepers", "A Poor Leper Woman Dragging her Food across the Snow" and "A Dog's Sagacity in Saving Lepers from Bears".

Her mission to the lepers is described in detail under such headings as: "Sinking into bogs", "Filthy *yourtas*", "Lepers carried on bare-backed bullocks" and "My entry into Yakutsk in a cart".

With immense determination, Kate Marsden risks her life and health, fights off bears and wolves, and braves all manner of hardship during a 2000-mile ride across Russia's icy wastes. Her mission is apparently rewarded, as almost a third of the book consists of letters from prominent personages thanking her and offering aid for her charitable work. The effect is slightly diminished by a range of advertisements for Dr Jaeger's Sanitary Woollen System Company Ltd (who supplied Kate Marsden with her winter underwear), Wansborough's Nipple Shields, and the Earlswood Asylum for Idiots and Imbeciles.

Ms Marsden herself in fashionable Jaeger travelling outfit, complete with flying helmet and Wansborough's Nipple Shields.

A Wizard's Wanderings from China to Peru
John Watkins Holden
Dean & Sons, 1886

Idle Days in Patagonia
William Henry Hudson
Chapman & Hall, 1893

By a remarkable coincidence, *another* William Henry Hudson was the author of *Idle Hours in a Library* (San Francisco, Calif.: W. Doxey, 1897). Idle lot, those Hudsons. . . .

The Avalanche Atlas
International Commission on Snow and Ice of the International Association of Hydrological Sciences (Natural Hazards)
Paris: UNESCO, 1981

The Little I Saw of Cuba
Burr McIntosh
F. Tennyson Neely, 1899

Hearts Aglow: Stories of Lepers by the Inland Sea
Honami Nagata (trans. Lois Johnson Erickson)
New York: American Mission to Lepers, 1939

Uganda For a Holiday
Sir Frederick Treves
Smith, Elder & Co., 1910

Perhaps the trip down Happy Valley was not quite all it had been cracked up to be, even then. The author concludes:

> ❛It is more than a relief to have broken out of the Jail of Monotony and to have escaped from beneath the heavy furnace-hot hand of the sun, while to see the white cliffs of England emerge from the mist is to see the dawn of a new heaven and a new earth. . . .❜

Weymouth next year, dear?

Yofuku; or, Japan in Trousers
Sherard Vines
Wishart & Co., 1931

Touring Libya
Philip Ward
Cambridge: Oleander, 1967
and:

Touring Lebanon
Cambridge: Oleander, 1971

Though possibly timely when they were published, in the light of recent events Mr Ward would have been hard pressed to have chosen two less attractive vacation venues.

13
The Greatest Novels of All Time
Fantastic fiction

To forestall criticism of the authors' selection in this category, they would like to point out that certain authors who have already achieved some degree of fame, such as Charles Dickens, Virginia Woolf, Evelyn Waugh and Graham Greene, are deliberately omitted from consideration for the Bucket Prize Shortlist.

The Shortlist: Our Top Ten

Hugging to Music; or, The Waltz to the Grave.
A Sketch from Life
"An American Observer"
M. J. Darg; New York: University Publishing Co., 1889; illustrated edition, 1890
A moralistic tale featuring Joe Jungle, the Wayback Infidel.

❛Victoria Lennox entered the conservatory on the arm of Deluth, as the latter exclaimed: "Deny it! Deny it if you can!" The dreamy, waltz-intoxicated Victoria was speechless. A grasp on the portière at her side relaxed and Jack Lennox fell senseless at the feet of his terrified wife. . . .

"Miss Rodney, will you honour me with the next waltz?" . . .

"Well now," said Aunt Sophronie as she tipped back with indignation, "why don't you speak plain English and ask me to hug you?"

Deluth looked ready to faint.

"Look at 'em . . . what would you call that if you had me in your arms 15 or 20 minutes without the music?"

"Oh, dreadful" exclaimed Deluth.❜

A sophisticated illustration from Hugging to Music *demonstrates the immorality of dancing.*

117

An Awfully Big Adventure
"Bartimeus"*
Cassell, 1919
(*The pseudonym of Lewis Anselmo da Costa Ricci.)
The title was altered from *A Scran Bag* at the request of the publishers in order to widen the book's appeal. The first chapter of these naval tales is entitled "The Wooing of Mouldy Jakes" – presumably also rejected as a collective title because of its use of another obscure naval term.

Tosser, Gunman
Frank Carr*
Ward, Lock & Co., 1939
(*Also author of *Two-Gun Lefty* (1940) and *Kid Sin, Killer* (1941).)

❝"Gee! If it ain't Tosser Smith. What are you doin' in this neck of the country?"

The cook stiffened as through his brain flashed the recollection of his recent attitude towards his visitor. His mouth became curiously dry. Tosser Smith, gunman, killer, outlaw. He'd heard tell that Tosser had killed more men than any other gunman known to the country.

Betty's fingers gripped her quirt tightly . . . she, too, had heard of Tosser Smith. . . .❞

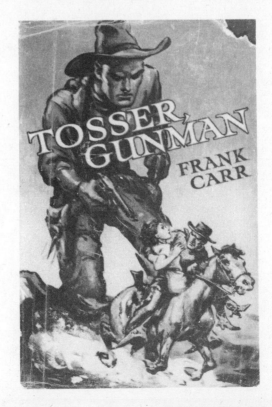

"She had heard of Tosser Smith. . . . She had seen him too. She couldn't really miss him. Tosser Smith was twenty-five feet tall. . . ."

THE GIRL FROM THE
BIG HORN COUNTRY

MARY ELLEN CHASE

Author of "Mary Peters," etc.

"The girl rested after her long ride and her thoughts drifted back to those far-off days on the Big Horn — with Tosser Smith...."

The Girl from the Big Horn Country
Mary Ellen Chase
George G. Harrap, 1937

A fictionalized account of the little girl who caused the celebrated battle in this elevated part of the world.

The Fangs of Suet Pudding

Adams Farr

Gerald G. Swan, 1944

His only book – but what a book! A wartime novel and the original "potboiler":

❛In the heart of France, May 1940 . . . Loreley Vance is suddenly awakened from her sleep by the entry into her room of, so she thought, a burglar. It may be that because he happened to be English, handsome, young and appealing, that she allowed him to hide under her bed, but whatever the reason it began the series of strange and startling events that brought her into the orbit of "Suet Pudding Face" Carl Vipoering, the master Nazi Spy, whose tentacles had spread over a small band of English folk who dared to oppose his machinations.

Even the addition to their party of two fleeing Dictators fails to quench the courageous and ingenious zest of the little band. They care neither for the dignity of the Dictator, or the Teuton thoroughness of a Nazi. How, in spite of "Suet Pudding" Carl Vipoering's most vicious efforts, they smuggle themselves and their two highly-inflammable charges out of the country, and

A title in the same war series as The Gums of Navarone.

perhaps, alter the whole course of the war, makes a story which will hold your interest and has all the bubble and sparkle of its native champagne.' (Publisher's description.)

'But Suet Pudding's fat, sunken-eyed egotism was not yet satisfied. If he had a whip I knew he would have cracked it. Instead he clicked his heels smartly to attention. And, for the first time that night, I smelt the stench of crushed violets. . . .'

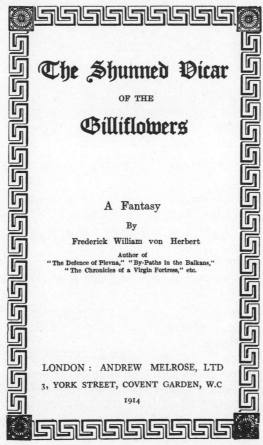

The Shunned Vicar

OF THE

Gilliflowers

A Fantasy

By

Frederick William von Herbert

Author of
"The Defence of Plevna," "By-Paths in the Balkans,"
"The Chronicles of a Virgin Fortress," etc.

LONDON : ANDREW MELROSE, LTD
3, YORK STREET, COVENT GARDEN, W.C
1914

The Shunned Vicar of the Gilliflowers
Frederick William von Herbert*
Andrew Melrose, 1914
(*Also author of *The Defence of Plevna, By-Paths in the Balkans, The Chronicles of a Virgin Fortress*, etc.)

In which the author useth the style of the Holy Scriptures to set forth how the Vicar of the Gilliflowers quarelled with the Judge of the village and eke with the people thereof, and could by no manner of means make peace again. After much travail, wailing and gnashing of teeth all round, the Vicar departeth from this world and the people take possession of his church with much noise and merriment, saying one to another, in their coarse language, "It's a jolly good thing the old crackpot's gone at last".

121

Groping

Naomi Ellington Jacob

Hutchinson, 1933

Although the author is perhaps better known for her earlier novel *Roots* (Hutchinson, 1931), *Groping* has been unjustly dismissed. It tells the story of Marcus Stern's struggle against adversity and his final victory.

"It is a curious and intimate novel; a small canvas painted with a wealth of personal detail".

They Die With Their Boots Clean

Gerald Kersh

Heinemann, 1942

Dedicated by the author to the friends "I got to know and love" in the Coldstream Guards: "I think that they represent all that is finest in army life". Undoubtedly, anyone reading even a small section of the prologue will realize just how effectively Kersh has portrayed their qualities:

❛"A man gets knifed. A throat gets slit. A bomb goes off. The Wogs are out for blood!"

As Sergeant Nelson talks his right eye blinks in the smoke of his cigarette. Pensively pursing his lips, he takes his left eye out, polishes it against the bosom of his battle-blouse, and puts it back again. "Is it in straight, Dusty?"

Sergeant Smith says: "A bit bolo."

Sergeant Nelson blinks hard. The glass eye stares rather angrily through the smoke. "You've got to close the left, or disengaged eye, when you fire," he says. "What's an eye?"

We wait, very quiet. We want to hear about the Wogs, the Arabs. Everything is coming. The moon is already out – a pale, thin little moon, no bigger than an eyebrow.

"Ah," says Sergeant Smith. "We used to see a bit of fighting in peace-time."

"Definitely, Dusty," says Sergeant Nelson, and his story goes on:

"The Wogs was around us. The desert was alive with Wogs. You couldn't see 'em. You couldn't hear 'em. But you knew they was there. They can hide, those Wogs can, behind a grain of sand. . . . Ain't that a fact, Dusty? They wears robes the same colour as the desert. They digs themselves little bits of cover. Puzzle, find 'em. You *know* they're there, but they're invisible. And the Wog can wait. He can wait hours. . . . Then *bomp!* – and *wheeee!* – he's letting loose atcha. He ain't a bad shot at three hundred yards."❜

Mated From the Morgue

John Augustus O'Shea

Spencer Blackett, 1889

Featuring French Legionnaire O'Hara and his friend O'Hoolohan in Paris before the revolution of 1870 "had wiped out the legend of the Empire as with a bloody sponge" – and without a hint of necrophilia.

Kinky Finds the Clue

Michael Poole*

George Newnes, 1948

(*The pseudonym of Reginald Heber Poole, also the author of *The Real Thing* (Thomas Nelson, 1930; reissued 1955), pre-dating Tom Stoppard's play of the same name.)

A superior detective-mystery tale which starts with the apparently innocuous purchase of a book from a second-hand book shop. Bill Quentin vanishes, and Hudson Mott (a celebrated journalist) is called in, aided by his friend Ken Kinsmith, "otherwise Kinky, who was 'something to do' with Scotland Yard. Kinky soon finds there's more to the affair than a missing schoolboy...."

Highly commended

A Romance of Bureaucracy

"A–B"

Allahabad: A. H. Wheeler & Co., 1893

A Queer Affair

Guy Newell Boothby

F. V. White, 1903

We All Killed Grandma

Fredric Brown

London and New York: T. V. Boardman, 1954

"From the very topmost drawer of Fredric Brown's writing table".

What Will He Do With It?

Edward George Earle Lytton Bulwer-Lytton

Edinburgh: William Blackwood, 1859

He takes four thick volumes to answer the question.

Not Like Other Girls

Rosa Carey

Bentley, 1885

Fanny at School

Frances Dana Gage

Buffalo, NY: Breed, Butler & Co., 1866

Gay Cottage

Glance Gaylord*

Boston, Mass.: American Tract Society, 1866

(*The pseudonym of Ives Warren Bradley.)

The Toff Goes Gay
John Creasey
Evans Brothers, 1951
One of The Toff's stranger adventures

124

Man-Crazy Nurse
Peggy Graddis
Pyramid Books, 1967

The City of Lost Women
"Griff"
Modern Fiction, n.d.
"Auction of Souls at the Point of a Rod. . . . A stark mystery that makes other stories seem flat and unconvincing by comparison".

Dildo Kay
Nelson Hayes
Boston, Mass.: Houghton Mifflin, 1940

The Bride Wore Weeds
Hank Janson
Gaywood Press, n.d.
"Best of Tough Gangster Authors"; also author of *Lady Mind That Corpse, Sweetie Hold Me Tight, Slay-Ride for Cutie* and *Honey Take My Gun.*

Gay Agony
Harold Manhood*
Cape, 1930
(*Author of *Nightseed*.)

Gay Agony

by

H. A. Manhood

Author of *Nightseed*

How Nell Scored
Bessie Marchant
T. Nelson & Sons, 1929
and:

Lesbia's Little Blunder
Frederick Warne, 1934
A pair of ripping schoolgirl yarns.

Gay Roads
Mills & Boon, 1936

Joyce & Jane
Mills & Boon, 1937

I Take What I Want
Collins, 1946

The Six Queens of Henry
French, 1937
Marjorie M. Price's enigmatic tetralogy.

Eight Years of His Life a Blank. The Story of Pioneer Days in South Dakota. A Novel
L. J. Ross
Waterton, SD: W. R. Lambert, c. 1915

Tombstones Are Free to Quitters
Ben Sarto
Modern Fiction Ltd, n.d.
The psychology of Sarto is to be brutal:
❛"I guess that guy got too much neck," Bigfella said. "But I reckon I twist it okay."❜

Every Inch a Sailor
William Gordon Stables
Nelson, 1897
The right publisher for this measured tome.

My Poor Dick
1888

He Went for a Soldier
1890

A Gay Little Woman
1897

Beautiful Jim
1900

The Man I Loved
1901

Magnificent Young Man
1902

Dick the Faithful
1905

A selection from the oeuvre of John Strange Winter (the pseudonym of Henrietta Vaughan Stannard), all published by F. V. White. As a woman writer masquerading as a man, she was, in the words of another of her titles, "Only Human".

Rejected as unsuitable on a number of counts

Assassination of Kennedy Considered as a Downhill Motor Race
Brighton: Unicorn Bookshop, n.d.
and:

Why I Want to Fuck Ronald Reagan
J. G. Ballard
Brighton: Unicorn Bookshop, 1968

Two early works by J. G. Ballard written during a period when the author's political beliefs were at the crossroads.

14
Against All Odds
Titles to make the heart sink

The narrowness of subject, unintentional humour of author's name or title (or both) or plain ludicrousness of many of the books dealt with in other chapters could qualify them as "no-chancers". But we have followed a more specific interpretation in assessing entry requirements for this part of our collection. Although some of them are, without doubt, excellent books, they have been given titles which make the heart sink. The title can be incongruous: *The Dream Palaces of Austria* – perhaps; but *The Dream Palaces of Birmingham* – ? Or it can be on a subject so inherently dull that even the most imaginatively optimistic publisher would have to admit that its "backlist potential" is about zero. The fact that some become bestsellers shows how wrong we can be.

Jokes Cracked by Lord Aberdeen
Lord Aberdeen (John Campbell Gordon)
Dundee and London: Valentine, 1929

SOMETHING FUNNY.
A young lady meeting Father Healy one morning, greeted him thus : " Oh, good morning, Father Healy. Now, won't you say something funny ? "—to which came the prompt reply, " Well, I'm glad to see you : isn't that funny ? "

Lord Aberdeen's original tart an' vicar joke.

'In the realm of Wit and Humour, Lord Aberdeen is a name to conjure with. All the kindly geniality of the North comes out in his rich repertoire of stories, and here the Publishers have pleasure in introducing to a wider public a few Gems from his collection.'

Companion volumes in the same tartan-bound series published by Valentine include *Stories Told by Sir James Taggart* (1926), *The Aberdeen Jew* by "Allan Junior" (1927) and *Hoots!* by John Joy Bell (1929).

JOKES CRACKED BY
LORD ABERDEEN

Cameos of Vegetarian Literature
Anon.
Ideal Publishing Union, 1898

If; A Nightmare in the Conditional Mood
Anon. ("By the Authors of *Wisdom While You Wait, Hustled History*, etc."
— i.e. Charles Larcom Graves and Edward Verall Lucas)
I. Pitman & Sons, 1908

New Teeth for Old Jaws: Bookselling Spiritualised
Anon.
Cole, 1826

The Romance of Tea
Anon.
English and Scottish Joint Co-operative Wholesale Society, 1934

Thoroughly Criticize the 'Gang of Four'
and Bring About a New Upsurge in the Movement to Build Tachai-Type Counties Throughout the Country
Anon.
Beijing: Guoji Shudian, 1979

How to Attain Success Through the Strength of Vibration of Numbers
Sarah Joanna Balliett (ed.)
Atlantic City, NJ: The Author, 1928 (9th edition)

The Joy of Cataloguing
Sanford Berman
Phoenix, Ariz.: The Oryx Press, 1981

'Twixt Twelve and Twenty. Pat Talks to Teenagers
Pat Boone
Englewood Cliffs, NJ: Prentice-Hall, 1958

A Frog's Blimp
Shinta Cho
Tokyo: Kosei Publishing Co., 1981

The Dream Palaces of Birmingham
Chris and Rosemary Clegg
Birmingham: The Authors, 1983

The Rubaiyat of a Scotch Terrier . . . With Drawings by The Author
Sewell Collins
Grant Richards, 1926

The song of a dog — and a dog of a book.

The Diary of an Organist's Apprentice at Durham Cathedral (1871–1875)
Thomas Henry Collinson (ed. F. Collinson)
Aberdeen: Aberdeen University Press, 1982

An Irishman's Difficulties with the Dutch Language
"Cuey-na-Gael"*
Rotterdam: J. M. Bredee, 1908
(*Pseudonym of the Revd Dr John Irwin Brown.)
Such was the success (it went through eight editions between 1908 and 1928) of this genial guide that a further volume was published, entitled *O'Neill's Further Adventures in Holland*.

The best-selling Double Dutch/Blarney, Blarney/Double Dutch Dictionary.

To Know a Fly
Vincent Gaston Dethier
San Francisco, Calif.: Holden-Day, 1962

SWEET SLEEP.

*A COURSE OF READING INTENDED TO PROMOTE
THAT DELIGHTFUL ENJOYMENT.*

BY

CHARLES J. DUNPHIE,

AUTHOR OF "WILDFIRE," ETC.

London:
TINSLEY BROTHERS, 8, CATHERINE STREET, STRAND.
1879.
[*All Rights Reserved.*]

A reviewer writes: "This book . . . zzzzzzzz . . . ."

Sweet Sleep. A Course of Reading Intended to Promote That Delightful Enjoyment
Charles J. Dunphie
Tinsley Brothers, 1879

By the author of the only slightly more lively *Wildfire* (n.p., 1876), it contains chapters guaranteed to beat counting sheep, including:

The Polite Arts of Yawning and Snoring
The Misery of Having One's Hair Cut
The Miseries of Development
The Pleasures of Poverty
Miniature Holland
On the Unimportance of Everything
The Delights of the English Climate
Pancakes

133

Ralph Edwards of Lonesome Lake

Fogswamp

Ruffles On My Longjohns
Isabel K. Edwards
Saaichton: Hancock House (trilogy: final vol. published 1980)

Wigan Free Public Library: Its Rise and Progress
Henry Tennyson Folkard
Wigan: "Privately printed", 1901

War in Dollyland (A Book and a Game)
Harry Golding
Ward, Lock & Co., 1915

Tells the colourful story of the battle between the Flat Heads and the Wooden Heads.

"The war fever is catching – awfully catching" – and it is a war in which no holds are barred.

❛The spy was led out at dawn. . . . He died as a brave man should.❜

A must for liberal-minded parents.

Just Ordinary, But . . . An Autobiography
Joseph Halliday
Waltham Abbey: The Author, 1959
Dedicated to "the average person".

A brilliantly realistic scene from War in Dollyland.

Hippy. In Memoriam. The Story of a Dog
Sir Nevile Meyrick Henderson
Hodder & Stoughton, 1942

In a year when most people had weightier matters on their minds, Sir Nevile Henderson (late British Ambassador to the court of Herr Hitler) chose to publish a biography of his dachsbracke, illustrated with several fascinating photographs, including "Sir Nevile Henderson with Hippy at a Royal Shoot at the summer residence of the late King Alexander of Yugoslavia".

Amor
Anai Imaya
Counter-Point Publications, 1984

"A small book of forty poems, but what poems! Every single one of them a masterpiece." (Emmanuel Gounalakis, Publisher.)

> 'In your Armenian landscape
> I want to explore every crevice in Yerevan
> Slowly climb the swollen Mount of Ararat
> And my arid mouth will drink from
> The lubricious waters of the gushing Arax.'

Working with British Rail
Hugh Jenkins
Batsford, 1984

Muddling Toward Frugality
Warren A. Johnson
San Francisco, Calif.: Sierra Club, 1978

A Letter to the Man Who Killed My Dog
Richard Joseph
New York: Frederick Fell, 1956

New Mexicans I Knew: Memoirs, 1892–1969
William A. Keleher
Albuquerque, N. Mex.: University of New Mexico Press, 1983

I Was Hitler's Maid
Pauline Kohler
Long, 1940

Follow Your Broken Nose
Honor McKay
Lutterworth, 1950

Dumps; a Plain Girl
Elizabeth Thomasina Meade
W. & R. Chambers, 1905

I Was a Kamikaze
Ryuji Nagatsuka
Abelard-Schuman, 1973

250 Times I Saw a Play
Keith Odo Newman
Oxford: Pelagos Press, 1944

In the course of the book, the author – who also wrote *Mind, Sex and War* (Oxford: Pelagos Press, 1941) – fails to mention what the play was, who wrote it, where it was performed and who acted in it. Asked for his comments, George Bernard Shaw replied in characteristic style:

> "I don't know what to say about this book. The experience on which it is founded is so extraordinary, that an honest record of it should be preserved. . . . But it would have driven me mad; and I am not sure that the author came out of it without a slight derangement. . . ."

Like G.B.S., we really don't know what to say about this book. Its author was also the "translator and adapter" of Baron C. A. Economo Van San Serff's Encephalitis Lethargica.

A Nostalgia for Camels

by

CHRISTOPHER RAND

An Atlantic Monthly Press Book
Little, Brown and Company
BOSTON   TORONTO

The unsurprising absence of nomadic camel-driver-library-subscribers in one of New York's most fashionable suburbs may account for this book's sad fate.

Children Are Wet Cement
Ann Ortlund
Old Tappan, NJ: Fleming H. Revell, 1981

The Wit of Prince Philip
HRH Prince Philip
Leslie Frewin, 1965

A Nostalgia for Camels
Christopher Rand
Boston, Mass.: Atlantic Monthly Press and Little, Brown & Co., 1957

By acquiring the Scarsdale Public Library's discarded copy of this book, the authors have removed it from circulation and thereby deprived the local jumble sales of their most regularly donated item.

The Mother of Goethe
Margaret Reeks
London and New York: John Lane, 1911

The English. Are They Human?
Dr G. J. Rennier
Williams and Norgate, 1931

Heroic Virgins
Alfonso P. Santos
Quezon City, Philippines: National Book Store, 1977

A Holiday with a Hegelian
Francis Sedlak
A. C. Fifield, 1911

Opens with a chapter on "What is Thought?" The author does not seem to have had much of a holiday.

Chancho. A Boy and His Pig in Peru
Sutherland Stark*
Redhill: Wells Gardner, Darton & Co., 1947
(*His only book.)

The Bright Side of Prison Life
Captain S. A. Swiggett
Baltimore, Md.: Fleet, McGinley & Co., 1897

(A Lineal Descendant of the Hereditary Standard or Ensign Bearers of Normandy and England from the Year 911 AD to 1309 AD When the Last of the Main Line Died Childless):
The History of the "Thorn Tree and Bush"
from the Earliest to the Present Time in Which Is Clearly and Plainly Shewn the Descent of Her Most Gracious Majesty and Her Anglo-Saxon People from the Half-tribe of Ephraim and Possibly from the Half-tribe of Maaseh, and Consequently Her Right and Title to Possess, at the Proper Moment, for Herself and for Them, a Share, or Shares of the Desolate Cities and Places in the Land of Their Forefathers
M. D. Theta*
Printed for Private Circulation, 1862
(*The pseudonym of William Thorn.)
The copy shown to the authors was completely unopened.

Along Wit's Trail: the Humor and Wisdom of Ronald Reagan
L. William Troxler
New York: Owl Books, 1984
"He has been called the funniest president since Lincoln." (Publisher's catalogue.)

Passport to Survival: No. 1 How to Lose £30,000,000
Elijah Wilkes
Routledge & Kegan Paul, 1955
Described as "A series of political pamphlets which analyse the evils from which our society is suffering today". Apparently this was the only title in the series published.

The Skeleton Edition of the Book of Comprehension No. 1
"The Preparation X.13: The Rose of Colour Reference for Technical, Kindergarten and Nature Teachers"
Frederick J. Wilson*
The Comprehensional Association, n.d.
(*Editor of *The Comprehensionist*.)
Incomprehensible.

The Mike & Bernie Winters Joke Book
Mike and Bernie Winters
Wolfe Publishing, 1970

15
Good Books
Unorthodox religious works

The Love Letters of a Portuguese Nun
Marianna Alcoforado
New York and London: Cassell, 1890

The Wordless Book
Anon.
Gospel Book Depot, n.d.

❛Small octavo 3 leaves inside, original printed paper boards, the openings coloured Black (Sin), Red (Blood of Jesus), White (Righteousness), Gold (The Glory).

Corner sl. rubbed, the Black (Sin) has two white spots (Righteousness?), the Red has a small nick off one corner, the White (Righteousness) is split up the fold, the Gold (The Glory) is sl. tarnished.

Words being dispensed with, this book uses the simplest form of communication – for a book, it seems an immaculate conception.❜ (Taken from the catalogue of Titles bookshop, Oxford.)

The Joy of the Upright Man
"J.B."
n.p., 1619

Rogues of the Bible
James Macdougall Black
New York and London: Harper & Bros., 1930

Becoming a Sensuous Catechist
Therese Boucher
Mystic, Conn.: Twenty-Third Publications, 1984

Hieroglyphic Bibles. Their Origin and History
William Alexander Clouston
Glasgow: D. Bryce & Son, 1894

Cooking With God
Lori David and Robert L. Robb
Hollywood, Calif.: Ermine Publishers, 1978
"Cooking with God is truly a labor of love." (Rosalyn Carter, quoted in the publisher's catalogue.)

Spiritual Radio
Ferdinand Herbert Du Vernet
Mountain Lakes, NJ: Society of the Nazarene, 1925

Modern Vampirism. Its Dangers and How to Avoid Them
A. Osborne Eaves
Harrogate: Talisman Publishing Co., 1904
Described as "a practical guide to those under threat", this invaluable book warns:

'With regard to protecting yourself generally, when rising imagine that a shell is forming at the extremity of the aura. Picture a white mist, ovoid, becoming denser every moment. Just as in winter the breath is clearly visible with each exhalation, so as you breathe outwards see in the mind the breath taking form. Use the will in addition, and this will have the desired effect. Repeat about midday, or whenever entering a crowd, or a low quarter of a city. At night again form this protective shell before going to sleep, and you are not likely to be troubled with Vampires. . . .

In walking in the street you can prevent yourself being "tapped" by closing the hands, as the fingers conduct the magnetism freely, and many people lose much in this way, which is lapped up from the fingers by astral entities. The body may be "locked" to prevent any leakage in railway compartments, trams, &c, by clasping the hands, and placing the left foot over the right, and thus form a complete circuit with one's limbs. Just as electricity discharges itself from angles and points, so in the human body.'

Twenty Most Asked Questions About the Amish and Mennonites
Merle and Phyllis Good
"A People's Place Booklet", 1979

Demonstration of the Spirit Originally Called Shouting
George W. Henry
Ottawa: Holiness Movement Publishing House, 1908
Mr Henry also brought us:

History of the Jumpers
Waukesha, Wis.: Metropolitan Church Association, 1909
and:

Shouting; Genuine and Spurious
Oneida, New York: The Author, 1859

The Manliness of Christ
Thomas Hughes
Macmillan, 1879

Mathematical Principles of Theology; or, The Existence of God Geometrically Demonstrated
Richard Jack
G. Hawkins, 1745

Scientific Proof of the Existence of God Will Soon Be Announced by the White House!
Prophetic Wisdom About the Myths and Idols of Mass Culture and Popular Religious Cultism, the New Priesthood of Scientific and Political Materialism, and the Secrets of Enlightenment Hidden in the Body of Man
Da Free John
San Rafael, Calif.: The Dawn Horse Press, 1980
"If you read no other book in your lifetime, read this beautiful, profound, disturbing, and hopeful book." (Worth Summers, Professor of Sociology, California State University, quoted on the jacket of the book.)

The Boo Hoo Bible: the Neo-American Church Catechism
Art Kleps
San Cristobal, N. Mex.: Toad Books, 1971

Esperança de Israel

Manasseh Ben Israel

Amsterdam: n.p., 1650

Promotes the theory that South American Indians are the lost tribe of Israel.

De Conciliatione Spiritum: von der Kunst sich mit Geistern bekantzu machen*

H. A. Matke and G. E. Hamberger

n.p., 1716

[*On the conciliation of spirits, or how to get acquainted with ghosts]

The Magic of Telephone Evangelism

Harold E. Metcalf

Atlanta, Ga.: Southern Union Conference, 1967

Traditional Aspects of Hell

James Mew*

Swan Sonnenschein & Co., 1903

(*Also co-author of *Drinks of the World* (Leadenhall Press, 1892) and translator of *Grammar of the Congo* (Hodder & Stoughton, 1882).)

Christ with the CID

Ex-Chief Inspector Reginald Morrish

Epworth Press, 1953

Would Christ Belong to a Labor Union? or, Henry Fielding's Dream
Revd Cortland Myers
New York: Street & Smith, c. 1900

The Beatles: a Study in Drugs, Sex and Revolution
David A. Noebel
Tulsa, Okla.: Christian Crusade Publications, 1969
A natural successor to the author's earlier:

Communism, Hypnotism and the Beatles
Tulsa, Okla.: Christian Concorde, 1965
and:

Rhythm, Riots and Revolution; an Analysis of the Communist Use of Music, the Communist Master Music Plan
Tulsa, Okla.: Christian Crusade Publications, 1966

Historic Nuns
Bessie Rayner Parkes
Duckworth, 1898

The Chemical History of the Six Days of Creation
John Phin
New York: American News Co., 1870
Phin later turned to less weighty subjects, including: *Bicyclist's Handbook* (1896), *The Preparation and Use of Cements and Glue* (1881) and *Trichinae (Pork Worms or Flesh Worms): How to Detect Them, and How to Avoid Them* (1881).

The Sacred and the Feminine: Toward a Theology of Housework
Kathryn Allen Rabuzzi
New York: Seabury Press, 1982
'An insightful examination of the theological dimension and ritual aspects of housework as performed within the confines of our traditional male culture. Rabuzzi also explains the thinking that can lead women either to denounce or defend housework.' (Publisher's catalogue.)

Ex-Nuns: a Study of Emergent Role Passage
Lucinda F. San Giovanni
Norwood, NJ: Ablex Publishing Corporation, 1978

Why Jesus Never Wrote a Book
William Edwin Robert Sangster
Epworth Press, 1932

The Sermon on The Mount in the Indian Sign-talk
Fort Smith, Ark.: n.p., 1890

In the Beginning Was the Word.
Unfortunately, It Was the Wrong Word:
the Chapter and Verse of Bible Misprints

The sixty-six books of the Authorized Version are divided into 1189 chapters containing 31,173 verses with 774,746 words composed of 3,566,480 letters, making it about ten times as long as the average novel. The task of typesetting, proofreading and printing such a monumental work was daunting, particularly in the days when it was undertaken entirely by hand. It is little wonder that of the thousands of versions that have appeared over the five centuries since it was first printed, a number have contained mistakes — sometimes of a glaring nature. Some of them have even become known by names derived from their errors. Among them are:

AFFINITY BIBLE
1923
Table of Affinity:
"A man may not marry his grandmother's wife"

BREECHES BIBLE
(The "Geneva Bible"), 1560
Genesis iii.7:
"and they sewed figge-tree leaves together and made themselves breeches" [aprons]

BUG BIBLE
("Coverdale's Bible"), 1535
Psalms xci.5:
"Thou shalt not nede to be afrayd for eny bugges by night" [terror]

CAMELS BIBLE
1823
Genesis xxiv.61:
"And Rebekah arose, and her camels" [damsels]

CHILDREN KILLED BIBLE
1795
Mark vii.27:
"Let the children first be killed" [filled]

CLAD BIBLE
1864
Matthew v.12:
"Rejoice, and be exceeding clad" [glad]

DENIAL BIBLE
1792
Luke xxii.34:
Philip mysteriously replaces Peter as the Apostle who will deny Christ.

DISCHARGE BIBLE
1806
I Timothy v.21:
"I discharge thee before God" [charge]

EARS TO EAR BIBLE
1807
Matthew xiii.43:
"Who hath ears to ear, let him hear"

ESTHER BIBLE
1823
Acts xii.4:
"Intending after Esther" [Easter]

FOOL BIBLE

1634
Psalms xiv.1:
"The fool hath said in his heart, there is a God" [Omitting the word "no" from before "God" was a costly mistake; the printers were fined £3000 and all copies were suppressed.]

FORGOTTEN SINS BIBLE

1638
Luke vii.47:
"Her sins, which are many, are forgotten" [forgiven]

FROG PRAYERBOOK

1778
Psalms cv.30:
"Their land brought forth frogs, yea seven in their king's chambers" [even]

HUSBAND ATE HER BIBLE

1682
Deuteronomy xxiv.3:
"And if the latter husband ate her" [hate]

Esther vi.2:
"kings of the door" [keepers]

Jeremiah xiii.27:
"I have seen thine adversaries" [adulteries]

Jeremiah xvi.6:
"neither shall men lament . . . nor make themselves glad" [bald]

Jeremiah xviii.21:
"Therefore deliver up their children to the swine" [famine]

Ezekiel xviii.25:
"The way of the Lord is equal" [is not]

IDLE BIBLE

1809
Zechariah xi.17:
"Woe to the idle shepherd" [idol; in the Revised Version of 1885, this became "worthless"]

INCUNABULA BIBLE

1594
Typeset by a dyslexic, it was dated 1495 (pre-1500 books are known as "incunabula").

JUDAS BIBLE

1611
John vi.67:
"Then said Judas unto the twelve" [Jesus]

LARGE FAMILY BIBLE

1820
Isaiah lxvi.9:
"Shall I bring to the birth, and not cease to bring forth" [cause]

LIONS BIBLE

1804
Numbers xxxv.18:
"the murderer shall surely be put together" [to death]

I Kings viii.19:
"but thy son that shall come forth out of thy lions" [loins]

Galatians v.17:
"For the flesh lusteth after the Spirit" [against the Spirit]

MORE SEA BIBLE

1641
Revelation xxi.1:
"and there was more sea" [no more sea]

MURDERER'S BIBLE

1801
Jude 16:
"These are murderers" [murmurers]

PLACEMAKERS' BIBLE

1562
Matthew v.9:
"Blessed are the placemakers"
[peacemakers]

Luke xxi (heading):
"Christ condemneth the poore
widdowe" [commendeth]

PRINTERS' BIBLE

1702
Psalms cxix.161:
"Printers have persecuted me without a
cause" [Princes]

Revelation xxii.15:
"For without are dogs, and scorers"
[sorcerers]

ROSIN BIBLE

1609
Jeremiah viii.22:
"Is there no rosin in Gilead" [balm]

SAND PITTE BIBLE

1534
Genesis xxxvii.20:
"cast him into sand pitte" [some pitte]

SIN ON BIBLE

1716
John v.14:
"Behold, thou art made whole: sin on
more" [sin no more]

STANDING FISHES BIBLE

1816
Ezekiel xlvii.19:
"And it shall come to pass, that the
fishes shall stand" [fishers]

STING BIBLE

1747
Mark vii.35:
"The sting of his tongue" [string]

STRAIN OUT BIBLE

1753
Matthew xxiii.24:
"Ye blind guides, which strain out a
gnat" [strain at]

STRAYED BIBLE

1824
Mark xi.8:
"others cut down branches off the
trees, and strayed them in the way"
[strewed]

Luke xi.29:
"and him that taketh away thy cloke
forbid to take thy coat also" [forbid
not]

I Peter iii.18:
"For Christ also hath once offered for
sins" [suffered]

TO REMAIN BIBLE

1805
Galatians iv.29:
"he that was born after the flesh
persecuted him that was born after the
Spirit, to remain even so it is now"
[The proofreader's comment "to
remain", referring to the comma after
"Spirit", was printed in this and the
Bible Society editions of 1805 and
1819]

TREACLE BIBLE

("Bishop's Bible"), 1568
Jeremiah viii.22:
"Is there no tryacle in Gilead" [this mistranslation of "balm" also in Jeremiah xlvi.11 ("Go up into Gilead, and take tryacle") and Ezekiel xxvii.17, and in Coverdale's Bible of 1535]

UNRIGHTEOUS BIBLE*

1653
I Corinthians vi.9:
"Know ye that the unrighteous shall inherit the kingdom of God?" [not inherit]

Romans vi.13:
"Neither yield ye your members as instruments of righteousness unto sin" [unrighteousness]
(*Also sometimes called the "Wicked Bible"; it is said to contain 6000 mistakes.)

VINEGAR BIBLE

1717
Luke xx (heading):
"The Parable of the Vinegar" [Vineyard]

WICKED BIBLE

1631
Exodus xx.14:
"Thou shalt commit adultery" [the omission of the word "not" from the Seventh Commandment resulted in the King's printers, Barker and Lucas of Blackfriars, being fined £300, which led to their ruin; only six copies are known to exist.]

WIFE-HATER BIBLE

1810
Luke xiv.26:
"If any man come to me, and hate not his father and mother . . . yea, and his own wife also" [life]

16
Peculiarities of the Press
Publishing curiosities and assorted trivia

An Awful Bind

What to do with a book with its covers off? Craft bookbinders are thin on the ground, and a traditional binding in leather is expensive. The amateur binder sometimes does it himself. The rich but eccentric collector commissions covers to suit the subjects of his books. Either way, the results can be bizarre.

Auto-destruct bindings:

The notorious B. F. Hardwick of Bradford has been justly described as "probably the world's worst binder". He flourished towards the end of the nineteenth century and certain features of his bindings can be spotted across a crowded bookshop. These include:

1. His use of half pigskin, heavily tanned, which reduces to powder with handling.
2. Neat trimming of the margins – often affecting the text area. (One of the star attractions of the 1982 Dud Books of All Time exhibition in York was a copy of Wordsworth's *White Doe of Rylstone* which Hardwick had reduced from quarto to octavo.)
3. Rounding of corners, thus further reducing the margins.
4. Highly durable imitation alligator-skin boards.
5. A binder's label that has a pronounced tendency to oxidize and disintegrate.

The firm continued until 1974. One of its last jobs was to bind Ruan Maclean's *Victorian Publishers' Book Bindings* for Lund Humphries. Ironically, at its liquidation the firm had a reputation for high-quality craftsmanship.

Black-lace panties:

Grand Opening: a Year in the Life of a Total Wife
Alice Whitman Leeds
Jackson Heights, NY: 1980

A one-off production. Pink satin, trimmed in lace; front cover embellished with black-lace panties with gun inserted.

Cigar-box boards:

The Soverane Herbe: A History of Tobacco
W. A. Penn
New York: Dutton, 1901

149

A choice of three appropriate bindings was offered by the publishers of this slim cricketing tale.

Coffee table:

Eboracum; or, A History of the City of York
Francis Drake
n.p., n.d.

❛A Unique copy. Drake, Francis. Eboracum; or, A History of the City of York. One of the very scarce large-paper copies. . . . Lacks the title page, full calf, corners worn and repaired with the brass edging and corners from a Wellington-style coffee table welded together by the son of the the former owner – who worked in a shipyard building submarines. A set of legs will provide the purchaser with the ultimate coffee-table-book. w.a.f. [with all faults] £245.00.❜ (Description from the catalogue of bookseller Michael Moon.)

Cricketiana:

Baxter's Second Innings
Henry Drummond
Hodder & Stoughton, 1892

We are privileged to have been shown three unusual bindings of the cricket book of Scottish theologian, Henry Drummond (1851–97). Two copies are in striped cloth in the style of a Victorian cricket blazer or a club tie, one with the title in the form of a blazer badge, the other resembling a linen name-tape. The third is a unique *pièce de résistance* – bound in off-white kid to resemble a miniature cricket pad.

Denim:

How the Other Half Lives
Jacob Auguste Riis
New York: Charles Scribners Sons, 1890

Originally offered for sale bound in denim from a workman's overalls.

Fishskin:

A copy of Isaac Walton's *The Compleat Angler* has been bound in fishskin, tanned by a process invented in Germany during the First World War by Hermann G. Schmid.

Greaseproof paper:

Alexandri Magni
Curtius Rufus
n.p., 1696

A fine example shown at York was sympathetically bound in "full greaseproof marbled lining paper with black Dymo-tape spine label".

Handkerchief:

The Love Sonnets of a Hoodlum
Wallace Irwin
San Francisco, Calif.: Paul Elder, 1901

Mr Irwin's "dulcet vagaries" are clothed in a rather colourful handkerchief.

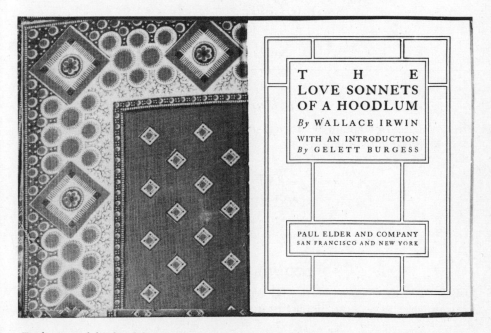

Each copy of this book has its own unique handkerchief binding. Trivia buffs will be thrilled to learn that Gelett Burgess, author of the introduction, was the inventor of the word "blurb".

Of Human Bandage:
God's Revenge Against Murder
John of Exeter
n.p., 1740

At York, an interesting copy of this work was shown. Featuring splendid copper-plates of stabbing, dismembering, garotting, etc., it was rebound in September 1977 by its owner, a gentleman of Bristol, in slightly soiled bandages.

Human Skin:
Narrative of the Life of James Allen,
alias George Walton, alias Jonas Pierce, alias James H. York, alias Burley Grove, the Highwayman. Being His Death-bed Confession, to the Warden of the Massachusetts State Prison
James Allen
Boston, Mass.: Harrington & Co., 1837

The Boston Athenaeum has the ultimate in autobiography – a copy bound in his own skin.

Leopard-skin throughout:
The Jayne Mansfield Story
Barton L. Beněs
New York: 1979

Malodorous edition:

The collection of Captain Maurice Hamonneau includes a copy of Adolf Hitler's *Mein Kampf* bound in skunk-skin.

Plywood:
Modern Plywood
Anon.
Pitman Publishing Co., n.d.

A rattling good yarn:

Also in the Hamonneau collection is a copy of Clare Booth Luce's *The Woman* with a rattlesnake rattle in the binding to warn off any reader attempting to open the book.

Sheets:
Rise and Fall of Carol Banks
Elliott White Spring
n.p., n.d.

Printed on glazed cotton sheets, bound in blue bedspread material from the author's own mill, and jacketed in little hemstitched pillow-cases.

Straw, alfalfa seed and a Webster's Dictionary (c. 1950 edition):

Two Sprout Books: Seed Thoughts
Douglas Benbe
New York: 1984

'Alfalfa seeds interspersed with straw pulp and shredded pages of the Dictionary. This mix then poured into deckle box or paper mould. The formed sheets transferred on to a flat surface where they were stacked and allowed to sprout.

Each day the pages were watered and tended. The intention is that the pages of these books open as a result of the growth of the sprouts and that the closing of these books will occur when they are no longer watered. As the sprouts die, each page will begin to close.

We participate by watching the process of their transformation over time.'

Uniform edition:

In the Hamonneau collection there is a copy of Erich Maria Remarque's *All Quiet on the Western Front* bound in part of a First World War uniform.

Wood samples:

The Schildbach collection contains samples of different woods made up by an eighteenth-century naturalist to look like books. One side of each volume opens to reveal samples of the trees' leaves, flowers, fruit, seeds and roots.

Strange Dedications; or, If You Can't Say Something Nice. . . .

An Essay on Silence
Michael Chater
Abbey Mills Press, 1969
A book of blank paper samples, dedicated to

'those who enjoy the sight and feel of good books, but to their sorrow have little time for reading them.'

Green Memory of Days with Gun and Rod
J. B. Drought
Philip Allan, 1937

'To the best bag I ever made in Ireland – My Wife.'

Alcoolisme et Absinthisme
Maurice Gourmet
Montpelier: Printed by Firmin et Cabirou, 1875

‘A la mémoire de mon père.’

Venereal Disease and Its Prevention
Felix Raoul Leblanc
Letchworth: G. W. Browne, 1920

‘To my wife this book is affectionately dedicated.’

Tristram Shandy
Laurence Sterne
York: Ann Ward, 1760

‘To be let or sold for fifty guineas.’

Memoirs and Anecdotes of Philip Thicknesse, Late Lieutenant Governor of Land Guard Fort, and, Unfortunately, Father to George Touchet, Baron Audley
Philip Thicknesse
Printed for The Author, 1788–91

Celebrated traveller and eccentric Philip Thicknesse abuses his son on the title-page of his *Memoirs*, but his full venom is reserved for the dedicatee, who had previously accused Thicknesse of cowardice during a minor military action against Jamaican rebels:

‘To James Makittrick, alias Adair,
Greeting,
As it is to you whose conduct I am obliged, for the very honourable and respectable names, which appear at the head of the following chapters; and who have kindly enabled me (without expence) to vindicate my character, and to defend my honour against a base defamer, a vindicative libeller, and a scurrilous, indecent, and vulgar scribbler; you are certainly the properest man existing, to address them to. . . .’

Clearly Makittrick found the attack so entertaining that he is included in a supplementary subscribers' list in Volume 2 as a purchaser of 200 copies of the book.

In ending Volume 3, Thicknesse delivers the final barb:

‘After having prepared matter sufficient to *bump* out this volume to the size of the two former, I have received a letter from a friend in London, who informs me that my *old friend* in Eton-street has, for some time past, been writing anonymous penny-post letters *to himself*, which he intends to publish as mine, in order to form a *fourth volume* of *my Memoirs*. And, as I am tired of writing, as, I fear, the purchasers of this book will be of reading it, I shall stop short here, and not deprive the public of the entertaining talents of a man who has been an old offender at the press. . . .’

A Bibliography of Books on the Circus in English from 1773 to 1964

Raymond Toole-Scott

Derby: Harpur & Sons, 1964

'In memory of my pussy.'

æt: 70.

The silhouette frontispiece to the unfortunate Philip Thicknesse's Memoirs.

Exercises in Making Life Difficult

The Greek poet, Tryphiodorus, wrote an epic poem, *Odyssey*, in twenty-four books, each one leaving out words containing a particular letter of the Greek alphabet. He started a trend for "lipograms" – works in which certain letters are deliberately omitted – which has been followed by such writers as Lope de Vega, who produced five novels each avoiding one vowel, and Gregorio Leti, who wrote a book without a single letter "e". Among other lipogrammatic books are:

Voyage Autour du Monde Sans la Lettre A
Jacques Etienne Victor Arago
Paris: n.p., 1853

The letter "a" appeared in the word "serait" in the first edition; this was corrected in the second. "A", of course, does appear five times in the title.

La Pièce Sans A
J. R. Ronden
Paris: n.p., 1816

When this was performed as a play at the Théâtre des Variétés in Paris on 18 December 1816 it somewhat taxed its actors and caused a riot among the audience, who did not allow it to run to its end.

Gadsby
Ernest Vincent Wright
Los Angeles, Calif.: Wetzel Publishing Co., 1939

With not an "e" in sight among its 50,000 words. Its author died on the day of publication. Wright was also the author of *The Fairies That Run the World and How They Do It* (Chicago, Ill.: n.p., 1903).

Then there are those who have gone to the opposite extreme, writing works where every word begins with the *same* letter, such as:

Ecologa de Calvis
Hucbaldus
Basle: Jacobus Parcum, 1546

A poem in praise of bald people, consisting exclusively of words beginning with "c" – and dedicated to Charles the Bald.

Pugna Porcorum
Publius Porcius*
Cologne: n.p., 1530
(*The pseudonym of Johannes Placentius.)

The book is written in Latin and all the words begin with the letter "p". After several hundred lines like "Plaudant porcelli, portent per plaustra patronum", this gets rather tedious.

And finally, Daisy Fellowes, the author of *Cats in the Isle of Man* (1929), attempted in her *Sunday; or, A Working Girl's Lament* (Monaco: A. Chêne, 1930) to introduce a revolutionary concept of poetic dialogue whereby the text is printed in black, red, green or mauve, according to who is speaking. This complex typography was clearly beyond her printer, and the result contains so many mistakes that every one of the 200 limited-edition copies has the appearance of a scrapbook into which are pasted odd words and whole stanzas of corrected text.

Editors and Printers Beware!

Strange Tales from Humlbe Life. Sold at a reduced price in Scotland only, by the Religious Tract Society, for behoof of the working classes.

John Ashworth

Manchester: Tubbs & Brook, c. 1874

A special edition with a cancel title apparently set by a trainee gravestone-cutter with all the traditional accuracy associated with that craft.

Strange Tales

FROM

HUMLBE LIFE.

BY

JOHN ASHWORTH.

——◆——

" The poor ye have always with you."

"The poor spellers ye have always with you...."

DEXTER'S PICKLE

FOR THE

KNOWING ONES.

"*I am the first in the East, the first in the West, and the greatest Philosopher in the known world.*"

The eccentric "Lord" Timothy Dexter gets his readers into a pickle with this book, which totally lacks punctuation.

Spelling and Punctuation Oddities

The Gates of Paradise
Jerzy Andrzejewski (trans. James Kirkup)
Weidenfeld & Nicolson, 1962
Although it contains commas, semi-colons and some other punctuation, the first full stop does not appear until page 158 – the last page of the book.

The Feminin Monarchi; or, The Histori of Bees
Charles Butler
Oxford: Printed by William Turner for The Author, 1634
Written in phonetic spelling throughout.

A Pickle for the Knowing Ones; or, Plain Truths in a Homespun Dress
Timothy Dexter
Salem: Printed for The Author, 1802
No punctuation.

The Elements of Geometry
John Dobson
Cambridge: University Press, 1813 and 1815 (2 vols.)
An impenetrable textbook with almost no punctuation.

Two Excursions into the Unnecessary

To the Curious: The Word Scissars Appears Capable of More Variations in the Spelling than Any Other
Anon.
Enfield: T. T. Barrow, 1829

This is not really a book, but a broadsheet, two copies of which can be found in the British Library; but as they are itemized in the catalogue and mounted in a book, we are taking the liberty of including them. The two copies are not identical: one lists 240 ways of spelling "scissars", and the other, by using double letters, has 480. Variants include:

> Sisszyrs
> Cisors
> Scysors
> Cyzsyrs

Why anyone should actually *want* to spell "scissars" in more ways than one is nowhere explained. One of the examples includes a woodcut illustration that appears to show someone attempting to pull down a church tower with a piece of string. Clearly the nineteenth-century mind was more agile than ours, as the publisher refers us to "the annexed Engraving, the meaning of which is obvious".

An Historical Curiosity, by a Birmingham Resident. One Hundred and Forty-one Ways of Spelling Birmingham.
William Hamper
Charles Whittingham, 1880

[Copyright.]   *Entered at Stationers' Hall.*

AN

HISTORICAL·

CURIOSITY,

BY A BIRMINGHAM RESIDENT.

ONE HUNDRED AND FORTY-ONE

WAYS OF SPELLING

BIRMINGHAM.

For example: Brymyncham, Brumegume, Brummingsham, Burymyngham – or even Bromidgome.

The Largest Number of Editions of the Same Book*
(*other than the Bible)

The Etymological Spelling-Book and Expositor
Henry Butter
Simpkin, Marshall, Hamilton, Kent & Co.

The first edition appeared in about 1830. By 1848 it had reached 111 editions and by 1886 no fewer than 442. The "new and revised" 1897 edition was not numbered but was described as the "Two Thousand Four Hundred and Thirty-second Thousand" [2,432,000] and there was an edition as recently as 1941; this modestly stated that 2,700,000 copies had been sold, but did not include an edition number. A frontispiece portrait in the 1897 edition shows Henry Butter, a bewhiskered Victorian with just a hint of a smile: he was perhaps thinking about his royalty cheque.

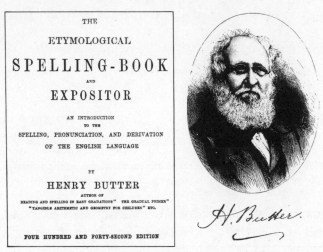

Henry Butter spreads himself over a record number of editions.

"The Funniest Book in the World"

Cole's Fun Doctor: the Funniest Book in the World
Edward William Cole
Routledge, 1886

‘30,000 of this Fun Doctor were sold in one part of Australia in about 18 months and 20,000 of them retailed in Cole Book Arcade, Melbourne. Mr Cole, in the public press, offered a bonus of £100 to any one who could prove that it was not the funniest book in the world or that ever was in the world. No one has yet been able to claim the bonus, for the simple reason that this is beyond all doubt the funniest book ever published.’

This extravagant claim is followed by 350 pages of the unfunniest jokes ever.

Best Example of Bet-hedging

In 1858 in New York John Worth Edmonds published two books: *Uncertainty of Spiritual Intercourse* and *Certainty of Spiritual Intercourse* (*Spiritual Tracts* nos. 4 and 5, respectively).

Longest Pseudo-initialism

In London in 1737 J. Roberts published a book by Arthur Ashley Sykes ("The Precentor and Prebendary of Alton Borealis in the Church of Salisbury") entitled *An Enquiry into the Meaning of Demoniacks in the New Testament* under the pseudonym:

"T.P.A.P.O.A.B.I.T.C.O.S."

World Record "Limited Edition"

The Man from Glengarry, A Tale of Ottawa
Ralph Connor
New York: Grosset & Dunlap, 1901

Special edition limited to 50,000 Copies

THE MAN FROM GLENGARRY

A TALE OF THE OTTAWA

BY
RALPH CONNOR
AUTHOR OF "THE SKY PILOT,"
AND "BLACK ROCK"

One of the 50,000 Men from Glengarry.

World Record Signed Limited Edition

My Philosophy

Elbert Hubbard

New York: Roycrofters, 1916

Limited edition of 9983 copies, every one signed by the author.

? & !!!

?

Sir Walter Newman Flower

Cassell, 1925

!!!

George Hughes Hepworth*

New York: Harper & Bros., 1881

(*Author of *Through Armenia on Horseback* (Isbister & Co., 1898).)

Special Award for Polysyllabic and Unpronounceable Titles

Le "Boschmannschucrutundkakafresserdeutschkolossalkulturde- struktorkathedralibusundkinden"

M. C. A. Kinneby

Paris: Les Editions Practiques et Documentaires, 1915

At eighty-four characters, the longest single word in a title – until some smart alec writes in with a longer one.

Runners-up

Logopandecteision; or, An Introduction to the Universal Language

Sir Thomas Urquhart

Giles Calvert & Richard Tomlins, 1653

Divided into six books with titles:

Neaudethaumata

Chrestasebeia

Cleronomaporia

Chryscomystes

Neleodicastes

Philoponauxesis

The Baron Kinkvervankotsdorsprakingatchdern. A New Musical Comedy

Miles Peter Andrews

T. Cadell, 1781

The Tragedy of Chrononhotonthologos
Henry Carey*
J. Shuckburgh and L. Gullivers; J. Jackson, c. 1734
(*Originally published under the pseudonym "Benjamin Bounce".)

Top Ten Unusual Publishers' Names

Aardvark-Vanaheim (USA)
Blubber Head Press (Australia)
Cum Books (South Africa)
Glad Hag Books (USA)
A Harmless Flirtation with Wealth* (USA)
Nervous & Mental Disease Publishing Co. (USA)
Rip Off Press (USA)
Strange Faeces Press (Canada)
Toothpaste Press (USA)
UG Books (Great Britain)
(*Publishers of Helen McKenna's *The Toilet Book: Knowing Your Toilet and How to Fix It* (San Diego, Calif.: 1975).)

A Peculiar Choice for a Pseudonym

A Bummer
History of the City of Chicastop for Ten Years, 1885 to 1895
Chicago: n.p., 1884 [sic]

Two Striking Double-acts

Bryan Balls and Richard Cox
Traveller's Guide to Malta
Thornton Cox, 1975

Robert Lionel Sherlock and S. C. A. Holmes
London and Thames Valley
British Regional Geology, 1960

Would You Buy a History of Canada by These Men?

James Maurice Stockford Careless
The Canadians: the Story of a People
New York: Macmillan, 1938

George MacKinnon Wrong
Canada. A History of a Challenge
Cambridge: Cambridge University Press, 1959

Serious students of Canadian history are still waiting for Mr Right to come along.

A Rather Inappropriate Official Publication

First report of the Standing Advisory Committee on Artificial Limbs 1947
Ministry of Pensions

An Interestingly Catalogued and Exotic Piece of Ephemera

EJACULATIONS.

Ejaculations to be used by a Woman during the time of her Labour.
London, 1853. a card; quarto
(British Library Catalogue)

An Uncommon Collection

With no explanation of what on earth it's doing in the British Library, the following item appears in the catalogue under "Collection":

'A collection of seven miniature volumes containing drawings of six beetles, nutcrackers, clay and briar pipes, horse brasses, scissors and candle-snuffers, American wall and shelf clocks and ancient musical instruments. The first drawn by Marie Angel and the remainder by Pamela Fowler. Bound and chained to a miniature wooden lectern which is encased in a cylinder, leather covered and gold-tooled. Executed at Froxfield by Roger Powell and Peter G. Waters in 1959.'

Silliest British Library Catalogue Entry

[Poems] [Edinburgh? 1785?] duodecimo. 11632.b.43.
Imperfect; wanting the titlepage and all before p. 17, and after p. 24.
In other words, a small, anonymous fragment, publisher unknown, date and place of publication uncertain, consisting of an odd eight pages from a larger work.

A Perplexing Catalogue Cross-reference*
(*British Library Printed Music Catalogue)

MUN (GEN OK)

– – *See* OK (Mun Gen)

Top Ten Rhyming Titles/Authors

Derwas James Chitty
The Desert a City
Oxford: Blackwell, 1966

Auguste Forel
La Question Sexuelle
Paris: G. Steinheil, 1906

Lady Winifred Fortescue
"There's Rosemary . . . There's Rue . . ."
Edinburgh: William Blackwood & Sons, 1939

Herbert Gold
Therefore Be Bold
André Deutsch, 1962

Helena Grose
The Flame and the Rose
Collins, 1954

Mrs John Lane
Maria Again
London and New York: John Lane, 1915

John Henry O'Hara
Appointment in Samarra
Faber & Faber, 1935

George Ryley Scott
Marriage in the Melting Pot
T. Werner Laurie, 1930

Samuel West
How to Examine the Chest
J. A. Churchill, 1883

T. H. White
The Ill-Made Knight
New York: G. P. Putnam's Sons, 1940

17
Last Words
Bizarre books on death – and after

The Practical Embalmer
Asa Johnson Dodge
Boston, Mass.: The Author, 1900

A Handbook on Hanging
Charles St Lawrence Duff
Cayme Press, 1928

This grisly book was first published in 1927 by Cayme Press in Great Britain and in 1929 by Hale, Cushman and Flint of Boston. Clearly popular on both sides of the Atlantic, it was revised and reissued (by John Lane) in 1938 and again in 1948. The version published in London by Andrew Melrose in 1954 is described as the "Definitive Edition". The 1961 Pitman edition is the "finally definitive edition".

How to do it – and how to stop it.

Duff (1894–1966), presents himself on the title-page as "Barrister-at-Law" and his book is "Dedicated Respectfully to The Hangmen of England". He advocates murder trials in the Albert Hall and Wembley Stadium, with the sale of film rights to trials and executions, the revenue from which, he argues, could enable the government to reduce Income Tax "which has always struck me as somewhat excessive". One section asks the question, "Why not hang in public?" Others, with titles such as "Hanging as a Fine Art" and "The Sheer Beauty of Hanging", suggest that Duff had something of a perverse interest in his subject. He would certainly have won few supporters among feminists with remarks like

> ‘we must away with sentiment, for it is universally recognised that, of all animals, woman is the most dangerous. Why, as recently as February 1951 a woman in New Zealand had the impertinence to apply for the post as public executioner. A hangwoman!’

This bizarre compendium concludes with Duff's "Ready Reckoner for Hangmen", which gives the universally valuable information of height of drop in relation to the victim's weight.

This book presents the best case for the abolition of capital punishment – as was undoubtedly the author's intention.

Sex After Death
B. J. Ferrell and Douglas Edward Frey
New York: Ashley Books, c. 1983

Deathing: an Intelligent Alternative for the Final Moments of Life
Anya Foos-Graber
Reading, Mass.: Addison-Wesley, 1984

Daddy Was an Undertaker
McDill McCown Gassman
New York: Vantage Press, 1952

The Art of Embalming
Thomas Greenhill
The Author, 1705
His mother, Elizabeth Greenhill (or Greenhille) is said to have had thirty-nine children.

Buried Alive
Franz Hartmann
Boston, Mass.: Occult Publishing Co., 1895

Hanging in Chains
Albert Hartshorne*
T. F. Unwin, 1891
(*Also author of *The Recumbent Monumental Effigies in Northamptonshire*, (Basil Montagu Pickering, 1876).)

Tell Me, Papa: Tell Me About Funerals
Marvin and Joy Johnson
Brooklyn, NY: Center for Thanatology Research and Education, 1980

Hanging Alive in Chains
Alfred Marks
Notes & Queries, 1909

How I Know That the Dead Are Alive
Fanny Ruthven Paget
Washington, DC: Plenty Publishing Co., 1917

Premature Burial and How It May Be Prevented
William Tebb and Col. Edward Perry Vollum
Swan Sonnenschein & Co., 1896

If you think that being buried alive is a fiction limited to your worst nightmares and horror films, read on. . . .

The authors conclude that "no evidence of death is really satisfactory except that which is supplied by putrefaction" and suggest the building of what they describe as "waiting mortuaries . . . furnished with every appliance for resuscitation. Only when the fact of death has been unequivocally established by the sign of decomposition should the body be removed to the cemetery."

The seriousness with which the problem was taken can perhaps be judged by the ownership stamp of one of the copies in the authors' collection: "Office of the City Coroner, Auckland, 8 July 1907".

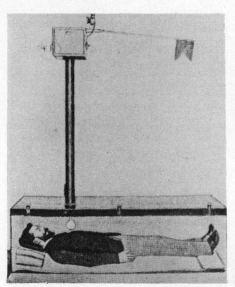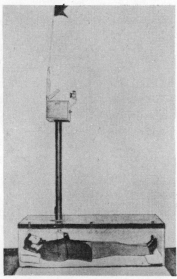

From Premature Burial: *If you wake up after being inadvertently buried alive, just squeeze the conveniently positioned glass ball which releases a spring to open the lid of the iron box, allowing air through the tube. This raises the flag, sets off a bell and turns on a light. The apparatus is "exceedingly reasonable in price" – only about twelve shillings.*

"Mrs Major, mother of three children. When she was hanged, her head was severed from her body." A plate from Violet Van der Elst's On the Gallows.

On the Gallows
Violet Van der Elst*
The Doge Press, 1937
(*Also author of *The Torture Chamber* (The Doge Press, 1934).)

Last Chance at Love
Various Authors
New York: Pinnacle Books, 1981
The *Terminal Romances* series.

How to Conduct a One-day Conference on Death Education
Ellen Zinner and Joan McMahon
Brooklyn, NY: Center for Thanatolgy Research, 1980

18
The Ones That Got Away
Elusive titles

We have endeavoured to confine the foregoing chapters to books that we believe to be genuine. Inevitably, we have been told about many that on closer investigation proved to be bogus, or less bizarre than they sounded. There are, however, a few tantalizing titles that we have heard about but that turned out to be elusive. We will be delighted to have them verified, and to receive further information and corrections to any of our descriptions – and especially pleased to receive suggestions, addressed to the Publishers (Bizarre Books Department), for further titles along the lines of those found in this book, for the second volume.

Anon. wrote to us with the following tempting information:
> One of my most treasured possessions is a copy of Young's *Night Thoughts*, 1853, sumptuously bound in full red morocco gilt, which has a pamphlet bound in at the end, presumably privately printed since it has no imprint, entitled: *The Dreadful Consequences of Self-Abuse* by J. T. Handyman. The fly-leaf is inscribed: "Phillip Fitzgibbon Fford on his fourteenth birthday from his Father, 14 Feby 1858".

Could Mr Handyman's first names possibly have been John Thomas? We have to know. Anon., please write again.

Here are a few others requiring further details:

Be Bold with Bananas
Australian Banana Growers Council

Crutches on the Go!
Vol. 1: "Amputees Above the Knee"
Vol. 2: "Amputees Below the Knee"

The True Inwardness of the Oyster
Devoe

Flashes from the Welsh Pulpit

Optical Chick Sexing
J. E. Hartley

How to Avoid Being Struck by Lightning

Reminiscences of a Clachnacuddin Nonagenarian
A. Maclean

My Single-Handed Fight Against Masturbation

Snoring as a Fine Art
Nock

On the Mutual Influence of Self-Excited and Excited Vibrations

Why Flies Buzz
Troughtoj

The Palingenesis of Craps
E. C. Tuiker

History of Freemasonry in the Province of Roxburgh, Peebles and Selkirkshire
W. F. Vernon

Who's Who in Australian Embroidery

The LITTLE THROW=BACK
FIRE EXTINGUISHER

GO ON READING
KEEP COOL————

Bizarre Index